Countryside Leisure

EP PUBLISHING LIMITED
1978

The frontispiece
is by David T.
Grewcock

EXPLORING WOODLANDS AND FORESTS

by SCOTT LEATHART

EP Publishing Limited

ACKNOWLEDGEMENTS

Dedication

To David whose work is in the woods

Acknowledgement

The author thanks Esmond Harris, Director of the Royal Forestry Society of England, Wales and Northern Ireland for his helpful suggestions

The publishers would like to thank the following for supplying the photographs used in this book and for allowing them to be reproduced:

Heather Angel, pp. 42, 43, 47 right, 73, 74 both, 76, 77; Archaeology Section, Royal Commission on Historical Monuments (England) (Crown Copyright, Central Office of Information), p. 19; The British Museum (Natural History), p. 10; Jane Burton, pp. 94, 98 right; The Forestry Commission, pp. 34 both, 78, 79, 102, 103 both, 104, 106, 107, 110 both; W. D. Fry, p. 63; Arthur Gilpin, pp. 82, 85, 86 both, 87, 88 both; David T. Grewcock, p. 92; Harold Hems, pp. 96, 100; Eric Hosking, pp. 83, 97, 98 left, 105; The Israel Tourist Office, p. 12; Miss Anne Jackson, p. 47 left; Scott Leathart, pp. 16, 25, 27, 29, 30, 32, 45, 51, 57, 58 left, 59, 61, 62, 63 right, 64, 66, 67, 68, 69, 70 left, 71, 72; National Maritime Museum, London, p. 20; Maurice Nimmo, pp. 8, 13, 17, 18, 26, 33, 35 both, 44, 58 right, 70 right; J. W. Porter, p. 48; Richard and Wallington Industries Limited, p. 28; John Topham Picture Library, p. 7.

The line drawings are by Ian Garrard.

The assistance of the Forestry Commission with the map on p. 109 is gratefully acknowledged.
The cover photograph is by Heather Angel. It is of autumnal beeches in the New Forest.

Copyright © Scott Leathart, 1978

ISBN 0 7158 0474 X

Published by EP Publishing Ltd., Bradford Road, East Ardsley, Wakefield, West Yorkshire, 1978

Printed in Great Britain by
Butler & Tanner Ltd, Frome and London

CONTENTS

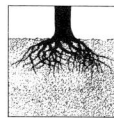

INTRODUCTION

Most of us at one time or another have stood high up in the mountains or moorlands entranced by the wide open spaces and the untrammelled views, as one ridge succeeds another to the horizon clad in the waving greens of bracken and the dusty purple haze of heather. Yet, however much a day spent in this majestic scenery may be enjoyed there is a sense that something is missing. From every angle we are exposed to the wind and the rain, and even sometimes to the sun; there is no shade or shelter, there is even a curious feeling of insecurity and often birds and animals seem scarcer and less confiding. But as we come down to the lower ground, we realise what has been lacking—the trees which we are inclined to take for granted until they are absent

The treelessness of the glen near Amulree, Perthshire, is enlivened by a number of bee hives

when, perhaps unconsciously, we crave for their protection. For we were once woodland creatures dwelling in the shade, shelter and security of the immense forests which used to cover Britain, and maybe it is an innate urge which attracts us to the woods. At the same time, we may know little about

A typical English lowland landscape with blocks of woodland, copses and hedgerow trees

them and the great variety of trees and wildlife which form these fascinating and beautiful parts of our countryside.

Historical events, as we shall later see, have reduced Britain's woodland area, as a proportion of its whole land surface, to a fraction of that in most European countries, and, as a result, there is not the same forestry tradition amongst us as we see in France and Germany. In those countries, and many others, communally owned forests, managed for centuries as places of recreation and sources of local revenue, are cherished by the people; the forest fastnesses, the trees with the timber they produce, the animals and birds, all are part of their lives.

As our forest area again increases so something of this tradition is starting to develop. More of us than ever before are

visiting the big new forests as well as the smaller woodlands, partly for the peace and quiet they provide and partly to see and enjoy the animals, birds and plants which live in them. One thing leads to another; we become curious. Why are the woods there? Not solely for our benefit or that of the animals and plants, but primarily for the timber they produce. What are these conifers and why are they planted in place of our native trees? What are our native trees? Why does the forester cut this tree and leave that? What bird was that which flitted through the trees, and why do the primroses grow here and not there? All these things and many more we may ask ourselves as we walk in the woods. The urge to explore is infectious and progressive; the more we find out the greater does our interest become.

Nature trails with pathside notices to help with identification, forest walks through woodlands in different stages of development, forest drives with occasional vistas framed by trees and forest parks with camping sites, are all giving us more access to the woods. From this we should derive a greater understanding of the complicated, ever-changing association of plants and animals of which the woods are comprised and also appreciate the need to manage them with care and sympathy.

At the end of chapters describing trees, flowers and wild creatures we have included their scientific names, for these are not just the tools of the scientists; they are an essential help to those who, in a search of better knowledge, wish to avoid the confusion caused by different English names used in various parts of the country, or of the world for that matter. Some may call a pine a fir, a cherry a gean, an arum lily a cuckoo-pint, a wood pigeon a ring-dove, or a polecat a foumart; but each has only one scientific name which, if looked at carefully and not avoided with the thought 'I never understand these things', can be both interesting and instructive. For instance, the wild cherry is called *Prunus avium*, from the Latin *prunus*, a plum, to which cherries are closely related and from which the English word prune is developed, and from *avis*, the Latin for a bird, because of the liking which they have for cherries.

So, in the succeeding pages we shall discuss the importance of trees to man and his fellow creatures—trees in their natural and planted communities, both large and small, which we call forests and woodlands. We shall trace the story of the decline of Britain's forests from their total domination over most of the country in prehistory to their scattered place in our countryside in more modern times and their restoration and gradual increase again today, primarily as sources of timber but also as habitats for wildlife and places of recreation. We shall see how the trees in them have changed with the changing needs of our population and how these changes have affected the animals and plants which live in them. Finally, we shall look at the more important animals and plants which we are likely to see on a visit to the forest.

The prehistoric fern-tree forests which once covered Britain probably looked like this

THE IMPORTANCE OF TREES

A world without trees would be a bleak place and life, as we know it, would be impossible. For some four hundred million years trees have been growing on this planet in various shapes and forms, and beneath their canopy life has evolved protected from the sun, the wind and the rain. The length of time Britain was covered by prehistoric forest in which lived dinosaurs and other strange creatures, can be gauged by the fact that 1½ inches of coal formed from the dead trees lying compressed beneath the ground, represents the accumulation of a thousand years; and some of the coal seams are hundreds of feet thick.

Just as trees in those far-off times were essential to the well-being and evolution of the prehistoric plants and creatures which dwelt amongst them, so in modern times they are of crucial importance to man and his fellow creatures. Yet, since he discovered fire and the use of cutting tools, he has steadily destroyed them, always for his own gain and regardless of the effect on him or on other living things. His forest clearances for agriculture in areas where seasonal droughts occurred created semi-deserts when water evaporated from the unprotected soil; whole forests, such as those of cedar in Lebanon, have been completely destroyed for building-timber; and succeeding civilisations, particularly in the Mediterranean area, have reduced huge forests to mere scrub in their quest for timber, the scrub itself being eliminated by grazing animals, leaving desert in its wake. In historical times, as we shall see, Britain's woodlands have been reduced to less than one-tenth of their former area. During the last century or so the great conifer forests of North-West America have suffered a gradual depletion, more in quality than quantity, by the consistent removal of the best and biggest trees, only the inferior ones being left to repopulate the logged areas.

Today we hear of avalanches, floods, landslips, droughts, dust bowls and soil erosion, all, as likely as not, resulting from the removal of the natural forest cover. If trees are cut from steep mountain slopes, the soil, which their roots bound together, is no longer prevented from slipping down, heavy with water, to the valley bottoms, tearing away fields and obliterating villages.

11

This photograph of the Negev desert shows the final product of tree removal

When trees are there, any snow falls gently from them to be evenly distributed beneath; in the absence of forest, this same snow is driven into drifts by the wind, accumulating in the bare upper valleys to fall in roaring and destructive avalanches whenever a thaw occurs. In warmer climates the destruction of tree cover has more far-reaching consequences, particularly in areas where there is a marked dry season. Here, extensive felling not only results in the degradation of the soil during the dry weather through excessive exposure, but when the rain does come it no longer falls gently through the trees onto an absorbent forest floor: it pours upon the unprotected, sun-baked earth running in rivulets across the countryside, gouging out great scars which become deeper and deeper each season. The scars join up to form torrents conveying with them the soil of the uplands and covering the lowlands in disastrous floods. And the whole process moves from one disaster to another; as more trees are felled so the moisture which they transpire into the atmosphere lessens and the rainfall decreases. The periods of drought become longer, the vegetation sparser and even more sought after by hungry animals until none is left and a virtual desert is created. Even in more temperate climates, and especially in areas where the land is flat, the removal of trees, and thus of shelter, results in extensive erosion of the topsoil, blown off by the wind. In a modest way we see this happening in England where the removal of hedges and hedgerow trees has been followed, in dry springs, by the whipping off of the topsoil and even of seedling plants, such as sugar beet.

These dangers we all now realise and much is being done throughout the world to put things right. In Britain we are lucky in having a climate without extremes. The destruction of our forests has not been accompanied by disasters, only by a deterioration of the soil in some upland areas and consequent waste of valuable land. Added

wildlife has logically progressed to an anxiety over the future of their habitats. Most creatures either live in woodland or, if they emerge from it to seek their prey in the open, need woodland for shelter, sanctuary and as a safe place in which to rear their young. So, in seeking to rectify centuries of destruction and neglect, and once again grow more timber for ourselves, we are at the same time starting to replace those habitats upon which so much of our wildlife depends.

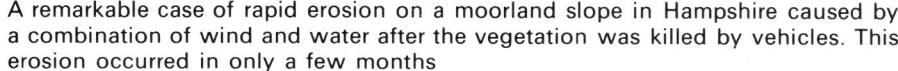

A remarkable case of rapid erosion on a moorland slope in Hampshire caused by a combination of wind and water after the vegetation was killed by vehicles. This erosion occurred in only a few months

to which is an ultimate inability to grow in our own country anything like enough timber for our needs, as well as a sad depletion of the habitats for our wildlife. We too as a nation are much more aware of the problems and what we should do to solve them. The need for timber is still very much with us (in 1976 we imported £2,154 million worth of it and its products for house building, newsprint and packaging and much else besides). We need to grow more ourselves. To this end large areas of moorland have been planted with trees by the Forestry Commission during the last thirty years, and considerable encouragement has been given to private owners to plant and replant trees. The felling of trees is now controlled by law, and permission to do so is usually accompanied by an obligation to replant. Because of much greater public interest, most of our birds and beasts and many of our plants are protected by law, and this concern for our

OUR ANCIENT FORESTS

All forests and woodlands are highly complicated associations of plants and animals, interdependent upon each other; and chief among the plants are the trees, specially adapted by size and longevity to be the dominant members of the association.

Like most plants, a tree starts life as a seed which, under the influence of moisture and warmth, germinates, pushing a stem upwards and a root downwards: the stem to bear leaves in the air and sunlight where they manufacture foodstuffs, and the root to anchor the tree and bring water and nutrients up to the leaves.

The life history of many plants is compassed in a single year; they grow from a seed, themselves produce seeds and then die. Other plants spend a year growing and building up food reserves, prior to seeding in their second year and then dying. Yet others die down each year but maintain their identity in bulbous roots underground. But trees and shrubs form stems which become hard and woody, persisting and lengthening year after year from buds formed along their length in which the following year's shoots and leaves lie neatly folded and protected from winter's wet and cold. Thus does a tree grow, annually adding to its stature, always with a head start over its less permanent rivals and, by virtue of the single stem to which it can devote all its resources, quickly outpacing the woody shrubs until, in the course of time, it outstrips all its rivals and dominates the scene. For millions of years this has been the case, and it is still so today.

Some fifteen thousand years ago all Britain was covered with a huge, thick, crushing icecap that had extinguished all the plant and animal life which had flourished so luxuriantly in an earlier warm period. Gradually, for reasons still somewhat obscure, the climate again began to improve and the ice started to retreat northwards, exposing afresh soil and water and thus providing conditions for plant life to regain a foothold; and the trees, with their special adaptations for domination, gradually asserted their ascendancy. At first, because of the harsh conditions, they were small and prostrate like the dwarf willows and birches still typical of Arctic tundras but surviving in Britain only as relics on the highest hills. Then, as the climate warmed, silver birches and Scots pines moved in, their wind-borne seeds covering new ground in annual, north-moving waves until they reached the north of Scotland where they still tend to be the commonest trees. These were followed by oaks, alders, ashes, rowans, elms, limes, cherries and aspens, all of which advanced north at least as far as southern Scotland; but a final group of latecomers, including beech, hornbeam, whitebeam, poplars and maples, came later, making much slower progress and extending only into lowland areas of central southern and eastern England.

As the ice melted so the sea level rose and, some six thousand years ago, the waters covered the land bridge which had connected South-East England to the Continent, putting an end to the natural colonisation of trees moving up from mainland Europe. Thirty-five species had managed to establish themselves in Britain when this severance occurred, but the sycamore and the Norway maple got left behind, as did three conifers—the larch, the Norway spruce and the silver fir. Later on, as we shall see, these laggards were introduced by man.

So, at the time when the British Isles could first be given that name, the country was for the most part clothed in dense forest. In the north huge tracts would have been covered with silver birch and Scots pine. In the lower-lying areas these would have been mixed, with birch predominating, whereas on the higher ground the forest would have been pure pine, or nearly so. The birches, as today, would have formed rather open woodland, with the same lovely white bark and drooping elegant crowns making the trees among our most attractive; but in those far-off times they would have been seen only by wolves, eagles and other animals which must have then abounded. Two species of birch are now recognised as native to Britain: the Silver Birch and the Downy Birch, the latter with downy twigs and prone to favour more marshy ground than the former.

The pines, with their striking reddish bark in mature trees and their bluish-green needles, would have ranged far and wide over the northern hills, tall and flat-topped in the sheltered areas, gnarled and stunted at the higher altitudes. Amongst them were groups of Rowans with their delicate, compound leaves, white springs flowers and massed, red autumn berries. Higher still the pines would have been more spaced out and beneath them were thick mats of dwarf willows and birches, covered by snow all winter. In these pine forests herds of red deer would seek shelter from the weather and wolves, and pine martens would prey upon the red squirrels. The Scots Pine is our only native pine, but is not, as its name implies, confined to Scotland; it ranges through central and northern Europe, right across into northern Asia.

Here and there in the northern areas there would have been woods of Alders on the river banks and lakesides, their dried, black, cone-like catkins clinging to the trees all winter; now and again their neatly chiselled, orange stumps would have shown where the beavers had been at work building their

Riverside alders often almost meet across the water

Remnants of the ancient Scots pine forest in Glenetive, Scotland

dams. In some places the alders would have been accompanied by groups of Aspens, their rounded, thin-stalked leaves fluttering in the slightest breeze.

Although the oaks would have been present in the north, they would there have been limited in their distribution and probably much smaller in stature than those of the lowland parts of England and Wales where the extensive forests would have been dense and composed predominantly of these trees. Bears would have had their dens in the fastness of the forests, packs of wolves would have run down the deer and sounders of wild pigs would have rooted out the fallen acorns. In summer the natural glades, carved out by lightning strikes, fire and wind, must have rung to the songs of many birds now only heard in continental Europe; but, oddly enough, there would have been no rabbits nibbling the woodland grasses for they were introduced by the Normans five thousand years later.

There are two species of oak native to Britain: the English Oak with ear-like lobes on the

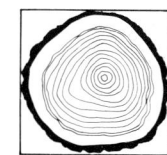

In ancient times oakwoods like this were the predominant forest cover in southern Britain

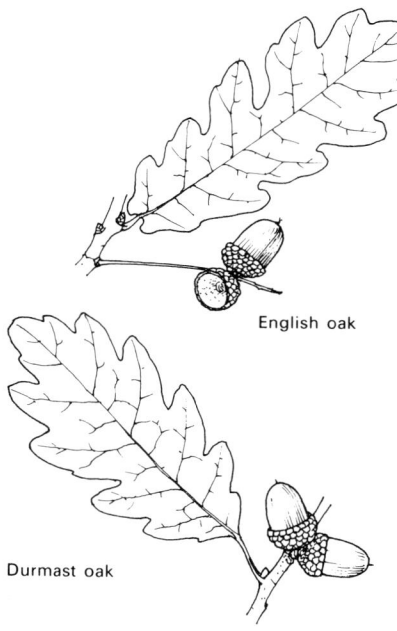

English oak

Durmast oak

base of the leaves and acorns borne on long stalks, and the Durmast Oak which has leaves without the lobes and acorns without stalks. The latter tends to be confined to the north-west and may well have been the dominant tree of the ancient forests of north-west England and south-west Scotland, especially on the lighter, hillside soils.

Of course, these oaks would not have reigned supreme throughout the forest. Other trees had their places. The Small-leaved Lime with its soft, heart-shaped leaves, would have found a place on steep slopes where oaks had fallen in the wind, and their hanging, green flowers would have been abuzz with bees seeking out the midsummer honey. The Wych Elms with their large, rough, lop-sided leaves, would have been present in the more northern oak forests where wind and exposure had retarded the growth of the dominant trees; and the Black Poplars grouped in low-lying parts too damp for oaks, would have added early springtime colour with their masses of reddish, dangling catkins.

In the southern half of Britain the forests of nearly pure Beech would have covered the chalky soils on the gently sloping Downs, Chilterns and Cotswolds in bright spring greens and autumn bronzes, their smooth, grey boles standing guard over leaf-strewn

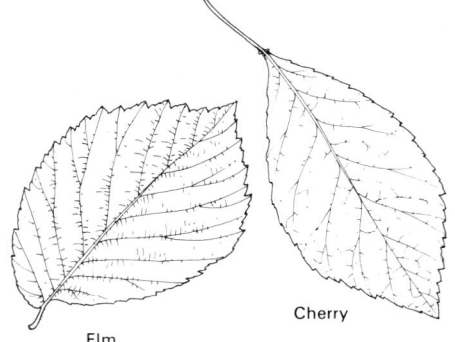

Elm

Cherry

forest floors all winter. In early spring the blossom of Wild Cherries would have shown fresh and white on the forest edge in contrast with the sombre dark greens of the Yews growing in groups beneath the beeches. Here and there, especially in the extreme south-east, the beeches would also have been accompanied by Hornbeams which look much like them but have fluted trunks and smaller, deeply veined leaves.

At this time man—if he was there at all—exerted no influence upon the forest. He was just another woodland creature, hunting animals and gathering fruits, nuts and roots in order to survive. For several thousand years the forest continued to cover at least sixty per cent of the total land

Forests of tall, smooth-barked beech trees replaced the oaks in chalky upland areas

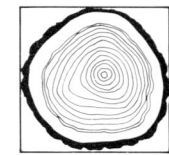

surface and suffered little change other than that occasioned by gradual climatic changes which led to fluctuations in the relative proportions of the tree species. But as time went on successive waves of Neolithic or New Stone Age men brought with them a gradually developing culture based on simple agriculture and the tending of domestic animals. These wandering cultivators, using stone tools to ring-bark and thus kill trees too large to fell, cleared small areas of the forest around the dead trees and protected their clearings with stockades of hazel. Beneath these gaunt, dead, leafless trees, which they were powerless to remove with their primitive tools, these early Britons sowed their corn and grazed their sheep and cattle. As the fertility of one clearing fell so they extended it or moved on to make another clearing, the grazing herds and flocks effectively preventing the regeneration of trees in those areas where tillage had ceased. Thus as men and animals increased so the destruction of the forest proceeded. In some areas villages began to appear,

Prehistoric settlements were in forest clearings protected by stockades similar to this reconstruction at Little Woodbury

particularly on the Downs, the Chilterns and the Cotswolds, where the beechwoods were more open and easier to clear and where, incidentaly, flints for sharp tools were readily available; but for the most part these stone-age men moved from place to place and so vast was the forest that they made but a minor impact upon it.

In about 2000 BC came the Bronze Age, an influx of people from Europe who had discovered that a mixture of two soft metals, copper and tin, in a proportion of nine to one, formed a much harder metal, one from which axes could be made. Forest clearance thus became that much less arduous and the tilling of the soil with new hand tools that much easier; it became possible to cut timber for building and other purposes. For 1,500 years

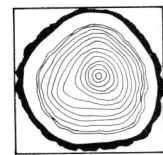

an intensifying assault upon the forests continued, leaving extensive areas of open pasturage where the hoe cultivators had done their work.

Around 500 BC the Iron Age was ushered in when Celtic tribes started to arrive in Britain bringing with them knowledge of the use of iron and all its accompanying improvement in tools, particularly axes. The most important development was in the plough, which meant that by the time the Romans arrived great areas of southern Britain had been cleared of forest and were cultivated. Even so, Caesar, in his *Commentaries*, describes the Ancient Britons as a true forest people whose military tactics consisted of hampering attacks which, if unsuccessful, were followed by a hasty retreat into the depths of the woods, the tracks being blocked with felled trees. The towns which Caesar described were merely clusters of huts grouped together for mutual protection in forest clearings, defended by ramps and ditches as well as stout fences of interwoven thorny trees and shrubs.

The 'wooden walls' of Britain—oak-built men of war

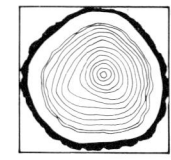

Throughout the Dark Ages the population grew, both by natural increase and by invasion. Anglo-Saxons and Danes spread across England, absorbing the Celts or driving them westwards and, being vigorous cultivators, they expanded, enclosed and improved the areas of tillage. With the advent of larger ploughs drawn by teams of oxen, larger fields on the heavier and more fertile soils in the valley bottoms became workable, and the upland areas were increasingly made over to permanent pasture. Thus the forest retreated and the wild animals that were destructive to crops, were driven into the remaining depths, great areas of which became something like sanctuaries for them. By gradual evolution these sanctuaries became reserves for the profit and amusement of the thanes and earls and subsequently for the recreation of the sovereign himself, subject to forest laws aimed mainly at protecting the game rather than the trees. By the time the Normans arrived in 1066, something like four-fifths of the ancient forest cover had ceased to exist, although there was still more than enough timber to go round.

The severity of William the Conqueror's forest laws is part of history, and the story of the royal forests which the Norman kings proclaimed, of which only two, the New Forest and the Forest of Dean, have retained more than a shadow of their former selves, is so well documented that one is tempted to assume that all the woodlands of England were in the stringent royal grip; but in practice these royal forests never covered more than a small fraction of the total area which, under pressure from land-hungry farmers and graziers, continued to decline. Nor was it only from deliberate clearance that the forest suffered. The main unit of medieval administration was the manor in which the right of pasturage was profoundly damaging to the forest trees; cattle, sheep and goats belonging to the lord and the commoners cropped the turf close and bit off the tree seedlings; acorns and beechmast were devoured by the herds of pigs let into the woods for their annual feast, and the right to gather firewood resulted in the decimation of saplings that would have replaced the ancient trees.

So, over the centuries this haphazard and insidious pillage of Britain's woodlands continued; less so perhaps in the north and in Scotland where the population was smaller. However, even there the treatment was just as damaging as conditions for tree growth were less favourable and such natural regeneration as escaped the enormous flocks of sheep (Melrose Abbey alone had some twelve thousand breeding sheep in 1250) was slow to reach a safe height beyond the attention of grazing animals. Then came a further threat, the necessity for charcoal in the iron-smelting industry. All over what remained of the thickly wooded areas iron furnaces appeared, devouring timber in ever-increasing quantities.

Although in Tudor times and before some attempts at the legal control of tree felling had been made, they enjoyed little success, and the alarm was not really sounded until the mid-seventeenth century when, as has so often been the case, the

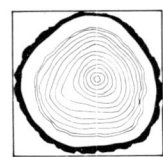

threat to national safety forced the powers-that-be to take some action. The growing importance of the Royal Navy as Britain's shield and the merchant fleet as her lifeline made great inroads upon England's oakwoods as more and more ships built of this uniquely suitable timber were needed. The old oaks were running short, a fact pressed upon Charles II who, through his newly formed Royal Society, selected John Evelyn to prepare a paper on the pleasures and profits of growing timber. Bringing a vast store of enthusiasm, a graceful style and what in those days was called a 'pretty wit' to his congenial task, Evelyn, in 1662, read to the society his *Sylva*. Printed in book form in 1664, this charming work became the first classic of British forestry Writing on his well-wooded estate amidst the charcoal kilns and iron foundries of the Weald, Evelyn knew only too well the value of wood in the national economy:

Since it is certain and demonstrable, that all arts and artisans whatsoever must fail and cease, if there were no timber and wood in a nation (for he that shall take his pen, and begin to set down what art, mystery or trade belonging any way to human life, could be maintained and exercised without wood, will quickly find that I speak no paradox) I say, when this all be well considered, it will appear, that we had better be without gold than without timber.

Evelyn's words fell upon fertile ground. At this time profound social and economic changes were occurring. Land held for centuries on a communal basis was increasingly being parcelled out amongst freeholders and the great estates were taking shape. Money rents and wages were being substituted for the old practices of services in goods and labour, farming prospered and the landowners grew rich and ready to heed Evelyn's call, as much from motives of patriotism as from self-interest. Much of the poorer land, unsuitable for agriculture, was put under trees—oak and beech in the south and pines in the north. Thus began the great plantation movement which, over the next two hundred years, was to give us the parklands, the woodlands, the patchwork of fields, hedges and hedgerow trees for which much of England is still justly famous.

Despite the enormous increase in tree planting and husbandry stimulated by Evelyn's encouragement and advice, the many new demands for timber, particularly for construction purposes as the industrial revolution got under way, could not be met. Not even the replacement of charcoal by coal in the form of coke did much to ease the pressure. Timber had to be imported, and it is ironic that although the new iron ships in which these cargoes came themselves lessened the demand on one source of timber—the oaks, they hastened the decline in Britain's forestry which attended the latter part of the nineteenth century by bringing in timber cheaper than that grown at home. Softwoods from Scandinavia and elsewhere were cheap and effective substitutes for England's hardwoods in building the huge new industrial cities, and our woodlands, unable to compete, once again became for the most part the unproductive sporting preserves of the rich.

The wheel had turned full circle crushing, in the process, some 90 per cent of Britain's forest cover and profoundly altering the landscape. There was plenty of gold but little timber, except that which had come from across the sea.

SCIENTIFIC NAMES OF TREES MENTIONED

Silver Birch	*Betula pendula*
Downy Birch	*Betula pubescens*
Rowan	*Sorbus aucuparia*
Scots Pine	*Pinus sylvestris*
Alder	*Alnus glutinosa*
Aspen	*Populus tremula*
English Oak	*Quercus robur*
Durmast Oak	*Quercus petraea*
Small-leaved Lime	*Tilia cordata*
Wych Elm	*Ulmus glabra*
Black Poplar	*Populus nigra*
Beech	*Fagus sylvatica*
Cherry	*Prunus avium*
Yew	*Taxus baccata*
Hornbeam	*Carpinus betulus*

OUR MODERN FORESTS

In the early years after Evelyn's call to arms the import of timber, mainly masts and spars for ships and rare timbers from tropical lands, did not seriously threaten the future economic viability of the newly planted woodlands because, with only horse transport available, it was very difficult and costly to move large logs any distance from the ports at which they were landed. So, the every-day demands of building-timber and firewood still had to be met locally and, as the plantations began to mature, so forestry flourished and went some way towards meeting this demand and at least lessening the drain upon the country's timber reserves. But, as we have seen, the industrial revolution changed all this; the enormous increase in population and in industrial activity could not be matched by an adequate increase in tree-planting, whilst the ready market for the goods which industry produced made it easy and cheap to finance the import of foreign timber. Furthermore, the advent of canals and railways made the transport of this timber cheap and easy. No wonder it became progressively unprofitable to grow timber in Britain and, in so far as the woodlands were cared for, they were maintained as sporting reserves.

Fortunately, there were amongst the landowners, both great and small, men of vision who grew trees for interest and pleasure and who sensed the dangerous situation into which the country was drifting through the absence of any concerted effort to build up timber production on a scale likely to match consumption. If it was apparent in Evelyn's time that a country could not live without timber, it was immeasurably more obvious in the mid-nineteenth century when huge imports of timber were required to meet the demands of industry. What would happen to Britain's industrial life if, for instance, the supply of seaborne pit props for the coal mines was cut off by war or an inability to pay for them? And it was not as though the country had no land available for afforestation or a climate unsuitable for growing trees; for at that time unproductive, rough grazing land extended to fifteen million acres, and had not natural forest once flourished over the greater part of the country?

The government was largely apathetic and reluctant to

A nineteenth-century parkland scene, with clumps of broadleaved trees framing the vistas

change its policies, such as they were, even in the old royal forests where some semblance of management and restocking a century before had resulted in a modest increase in the supply of special oak timber for shipbuilding, now no longer required. So the landowners rightly conceived it their duty to urge a remedy upon successive governments, and they did this as much by example as by protestation.

It was obvious that a situation that had deteriorated by default over so many years could not be corrected quickly by planting solely the slow-growing native hardwoods; indeed, the demands of the industrial revolution were only being met by the import of relatively quick-grown softwoods of which there was a seemingly inexhaustable supply from northern Europe. So the landowners tended to concentrate on the planting of conifers and their scope was greatly extended by the discovery of the north-west American conifers of which they established trial plantations. It soon became apparent that many of these trees did remarkably well in Britain and that even the European species such as larch and spruce grew much quicker in our oceanic climate than in their native lands. It was also discovered that many of these conifers would grow on former woodland sites and soils, impoverished by felling and neglect, where native trees failed to re-establish themselves. Some of these exotic trees not only provided an early return of timber but, when planted in mixture with oak and beech, also gave protection to the young hardwoods and improved their ultimate quality.

All these discoveries and the enthusiasm which prompted and accompanied them were disseminated in the official publications of the newly formed Royal Scottish Forestry Society (1854) and the Royal English Arboricultural Society (1882), both societies instituted by small groups of woodland owners and their

Nineteenth-century landscape architects incorporated exotic conifers in their designs

employees. These societies held outdoor meetings up and down the country at which members visited woodlands for demonstrations and discussions; always the main theme was how could the huge areas of unproductive woodland be rehabilitated to forestall the timber shortage which they saw coming? How could they introduce more scientific methods to forestry to help this process? And how could those who managed the woods and worked in them be trained more scientifically? Once again, as in the days of the formation of the Royal Society, it was a small band of private individuals who took the initiative whilst the government looked no farther than the end of its nose.

As the years unfolded a modicum of renewal took place. Old, neglected coppice, good only for holding pheasants, was replaced by mixed hardwood and conifer woodland; bare hillsides took on coats of spruce and larch, and selective fellings in the beechwoods ensured a constant succession of younger trees. The countryside of Britain, always to some extent influenced by the prevailing economic circumstances, began to take on a new aspect. Where in winter leafless hardwoods had predominated in unbroken grey, evergreen conifers added variety to the scene; where stunted oak had filled a valley in unproductive and gnarled monotony, tall, bright green Douglas firs reached for the sky, and around the mansions and in the old deer parks the clumps of beech and oak were overtopped by wellingtonias or flanked by spreading cedars. Gradually, the woodlands of old were starting to flourish anew. Even the government, through the Office of Woods, Forests and Land Revenue, in a small way began reafforestation beyond the bounds of the old royal forests.

Then the Great War struck, amply justifying all the grim forebodings. The German submarine campaign very soon imperilled the supply of pit props and other timber vital to

the war effort. Great areas of woodland, so carefully tended by those private owners who had sounded the largely unheeded alarm, had to be clear-felled without any regard to the conservation of future supplies, and by the time the war ended Britain's woodlands had been reduced by nearly half a million acres.

So great was the concern felt for the future that in 1917 a committee under Sir Richard Acland was set up, charged with investigating how best Britain's forestry could be given an assured long-term future. It recommended the establishment of a national forest authority and, in 1919, the Forestry Commission was born with the appointed task of planting up 200,000 acres of waste land in ten years, and up to 1,770,000 acres by the end of the century.

The new Commission proved more than able to meet the immediate target. By 1939 and the start of the Second World War, 230 new forests, covering some 655,000 acres of woodland and potentially plantable land, had been established and of these nearly 360,000 acres had actually

been planted—mostly with coniferous trees on land in upland areas of little value for agriculture. But, of course, no trees in these new forests were more than twenty years old and they could contribute little to the timber demands of this second national emergency. Again the burden fell upon the private owners. Fewer than the government complacently expected had managed to rehabilitate their devastated woodlands but most of them

still had considerable acreages of usable timber established by their far-sighted and patriotic forebears.

For six years the axes rang throughout the land, clear-felling 373,000 acres and devastating a further 150,000 by the removal of the better trees from amongst those of lesser quality and stature.

It thus became clear that timber would always have a vital part to play both in the defence of the realm and in its

A graded beech log being loaded onto a trailer for transport to a furniture factory in High Wycombe

Tree-length sawlogs are easily lifted onto a trailer in the woods by this hydraulic Monda 64 crane

economic well-being, and that not only would the state have to play a more active part itself in planting and managing woodlands but that it was also morally bound to assist private owners to repair their losses. Furthermore, self-interest demanded that the state should in future give financial support to such owners as were prepared to invest in forestry. So a target was set of five million acres (an increase of three million) of productive forest, both state and private, by the end of the century. The owners were to be encouraged by cash grants and tax concessions, and this forest estate was eventually to produce some 35 per cent of our total requirements and to provide a strategic reserve.

Assistance to private forestry was given under a scheme whereby an owner, in return for agreeing to keep certain parts of his estate under productively managed woodland in perpetuity and in accordance with a plan approved by the Forestry Commission, would be eligible for a grant of money on an acreage basis towards the planting of trees and a subsequent annual maintenance grant to ensure their proper care. Owners thus 'dedicated' their existing woodlands or land designated for tree-planting to timber production, and this admirable method of encouraging tree-planting and woodland maintenance, known as the Dedication Scheme, has proved a great success. Since its inception in 1947 it has played a significant part in helping to increase the country's forestry investment. There are now nearly 1,300,000 acres of dedicated private woodland (as well as a further 170,000 acres of 'approved woodland', a less permanent but similarly grant-aided scheme), and these together with the Forestry Commission's total forest area of 2,040,000 acres show what good progress is being made towards the five million target.

Thus, in the last three decades we have seen a fruitful partnership between state and private forestry with the

A charming mixture of exotic and native trees in the Happy Valley woodland garden at Redleaf, Kent

Commission acting in a dual capacity: as the state forest service managing Britain's two million acres of publicly owned forests, and as the national forest authority advising private owners and supervising the scheme which gives them financial assistance. By this partnership the government are able to ensure that the country's private woodlands, and particularly England's broad-leaved woods, most of which are in private hands, are restored and maintained without actually having to become involved in their day-to-day management; and the owners, who after all have very nearly half of the country's woodlands in their care, are able to draw upon the advice, research and technical know-how of the Commission. As a result and in addition to the expansion of our forests, there has been a marked improvement in their overall quality and thus a much better use of our land, which in these small islands is at a considerable premium.

In upland areas, particularly in the west and on soils impoverished by over-grazing and neglect, we now have forests of spruce which, although they occupy land once supporting sheep, often so shelter the remaining moorland that it can support as many or more sheep in the reduced area. In steep-sided valleys useless for agriculture, where scrub oak gave no return and little visual pleasure except to those who see beauty in the fag-end of nature's forlorn attempts to right years of greed and neglect, we see larch nursing beneath their light canopy oaks which will in time restore the valleys to their earlier beauty. On sandy heaths, reduced by rabbits to open, windswept areas of gorse or heather and rushes, pines now protect the light soils from the excesses of sun, wind and rain, helping it to regain some of its former fertility. On the chalky Chilterns, Downs and Cotswolds the aging beeches left after wartime fellings now have young trees of their own kind beneath them in

conifer forests, will come to consider them as a natural part of our countryside.

A mixed woodland of native hardwoods, with Christmas trees planted in a clearing

successive age classes, some planted, others natural seedlings left in groups where needed, but all according to the foresters' plans to keep the woods in permanent production without destroying the protective canopy. On the lowland clays the oakwoods are growing up again interspersed with plantations of larch, spruce, Douglas fir and, to a lesser extent, other species such as western hemlock. And many variations on all these themes, according to soil and site, all with one object—to grow timber. That in so doing these ever-changing woodlands also provide habitats for wildlife and quiet recreation areas for ourselves is a bonus to be discussed later, and even though the older among us may regret the partial eclipse of our native hardwoods, the younger generation accustomed from childhood to the new

THE PRACTICE OF FORESTRY

The land area of Britain is too small, with too many people living in it, for us to leave with impunity any significant portion of it in unproductive neglect. It must either grow things to eat and use, support buildings or provide areas for recreation. That is why our woodlands and forests must be used mainly for the growing of timber or for the provision of shelter for crops and animals. This is not to say that all our forests must be of quick-growing conifers or that we should pay no heed to the effect of tree-planting on the landscape, or that we should neglect the needs of the wonderfully varied woodland wildlife that we hold in trust for future generations; but it does mean that, by and large, the sites and soils available for tree-planting should be stocked with those trees which will

grow best on them. For instance, where poor hardwoods, often the end-product of past bad management, can no longer produce usable timber it is better to remove and replace them with conifers that will thrive on the relatively impoverished soil, grow good timber and at the same time improve the soil so that in future years hardwoods may once again be planted. True, a habitat for certain groups of plants and animals may go, but another for others will be created and, in any case, few foresters will be averse to leaving small areas of the old tree cover as reserves. So, assuming that the great majority of woodlands are there for the production of timber, and are thus in the care of foresters, let us see how they

are managed for this purpose and, later on, what form they take and for what sorts of wildlife they provide such varied and essential habitats.

Forestry is basically the growing of trees for the production of timber by influencing, assisting and even at times combating Nature. In Britain this practice started hundreds of years ago when natural saplings that provided the small poles, so essential for many uses in those days, became scarce due to over-cutting and over-grazing. This early manifestation of systematic forestry was called *coppice* from the French 'coupe', to cut; the trees were cut at ground level at regular intervals when several shoots sprouted from the stumps to give the required poles. This cutting was repeated every ten

years or so, the intervals between the cuttings being the *rotation*. A regular supply and a known quantity of poles was ensured by dividing the wood into a number of equal areas or *compartments*, the number being the same as the years of the rotation. So, a hundred-acre wood on a ten-year rotation, divided into ten compartments, one compartment being cut annually, would ensure a regular supply of poles indefinitely as the first to be cut would again be ready for harvesting when the tenth had been cut. This coppice crop, usually hazel, oak, ash or hornbeam, was very valuable in those days as the raw material of skilled craftsmen such as hurdle-makers, cleavers, turners and bark-strippers, with the waste going for firewood. Wherever on maps the woodland names contain the words 'copse' it is safe to assume that they were at one time managed in this way. Some old coppice woodland still exists to this day, easily recognised by the several trunks which spring from the single and often much decayed stumps; but for the most part

A hurdle-maker, using hazel rods from coppice woodland, demonstrates his craft at the Bath and West Show

they have been converted into something more profitable and in keeping with the times.

As the larger timber also became scarce a different system incorporating the coppice but including uncut trees, called *coppice-with-standards*, was introduced. Isolated timber trees, usually oak or ash, were left to grow to their full stature in the midst of the coppice growth, so that after, say, ten rotations of ten years they would have reached good timber size and could then be felled for the many uses for which large dimensions were required. But, being isolated and without competition from other trees, they tended to produce wide-spreading crowns on short, branchy trunks restricting the length of the timber, as opposed to the bulk, although the thick, crooked branches were invaluable for shipbuilding. As timber length was important, this fact

Coppiced hazels with standard oaks amongst them

combined with the drawback that the coppice beneath the standard trees was often suppressed, made the system uneconomic in more modern times, and now almost totally obsolete—although areas still persisted, often in dereliction and neglect, even after the last war. Some evidence of the old, spreading trees can still be found in older woodland in southern England.

Nowadays, in one form or another, forestry has returned to what Nature ultimately always provides—*high forest*. The trees are allowed to grow up together and compete with one another. In the natural course of things, disease, wind and genetic debility eventually single out the weakling trees, leaving the best to reach maturity. In systematic forestry the forester cuts out, or *thins*, those trees which he considers are unlikely to prosper or which, by competing with the better trees, will impede their growth. For, on a given area of land only a given volume of timber can be grown, either in many small trees or in fewer larger ones; and as the usual requirement is big timber, the trees to produce this, the *final crop*, must have enough space between them to permit ample development. This does not mean that after a few years or as soon as the best trees are discernible, all competing trees are thinned at one time. The process must be gradual, as in Nature, both to keep the wind from blowing down the chosen trees and to guard the forest floor from excessive exposure. This also prevents the final crop trees from branching out like the standards in the old coppice areas, and, incidentally, evens out the supply of the smaller timber which the thinnings produce and upon the sale of which the forester relies to pay for the establishment and upkeep of the crop. So he conducts his thinning operations over a period of many years, according to the species of trees and thus the rotation, and thins lightly or heavily according to the needs of the trees and the markets currently available for the produce. The factors that

Thinnings from a conifer plantation are ferried to the roadside by a tractor-mounted winch

unlikely to prosper as well as another smaller specimen nearby. Always he must try to offset the danger of opening up the canopy too much too quickly against the necessity of allowing the individual trees sufficient space in which to develop their individual crowns, without which they cannot put on timber.

The trunk of a tree expands annually by the addition of a new layer of wood added to the circumference each spring and summer; so the forester, by measuring the diameter or circumference at regular intervals, can tell how quickly the tree is growing. From this he will learn how the tree is responding to his thinning programme which, as we have

influence him in deciding how many and which trees to remove are many: the position of the trees, their general shape and form; whether a badly shaped and poorly developed specimen is in some measure of competition with a well-formed neighbour; whether a damaged tree, although in other respects promising, is

The diameter and length of a felled oak tree are measured to give volume

that the forester's activities are aimed. Obviously, in a large area of woodland he cannot measure every tree, so he marks out a sample plot of a known area in a part of the wood where the trees show average growth, and measures all the trees in this plot; from this data he can estimate the increment of the whole crop.

High forest, once felled, may be re-established by natural or artificial means: that is by

A cross-section of an oak stem shows the rings of wood added annually to the trunk. The converging medullary rays give oak its unique figuring

seen, is designed to encourage the chosen trees to put on as much girth (timber) as possible. These measurements, together with those of the length and taper of the trunk, will also enable him to calculate the total volume of timber in each tree and thus of the whole plantation. The increase in volume each year is called the *annual increment*, and it is to maintain this increase at an optimum amount

Young beech trees growing up beneath their parents

natural seeding or by artificial sowing or planting. In practice the former method is rarely used in Britain, except in the case of some beech- and pinewoods, because plentiful crops of seed occur only at long and irregular intervals, apparently after those rare long, hot summers; but when possible it is a cheap and easy method. In the case of hardwoods the usual method is to leave a number of seed or mother trees well spaced over the felled area from which the seed, when it comes, will be more or less evenly scattered. With pines and spruce, which seed more frequently, strips are cut downwind of the standing trees from which the seeds are blown on to the vacant ground. The mass of seedlings resulting from these methods is then allowed to grow in competition, each drawing up the other until the forester deems it time to start his thinning programme.

A more usual method employed, one that is unavoidable in afforestation, is the planting of transplants from a forest nursery. The small trees, evenly spaced apart in straight lines, are planted in winter or early spring when they are dormant. It is neither physically nor financially possible to plant trees as thickly as Nature can sow them, so the spaces between them quickly become filled with other competing plants. Having the trees in straight lines in known positions is the only system which will enable the forester to cut away the competing weeds, either by hand or machine, without harming the trees.

These little trees, like all young things, need protection. Where rabbits, hares, deer and domestic animals, particularly sheep, abound they may need fencing in. In some areas, particularly the boggy uplands or where old trees have been felled and no longer pump water out of the ground, drains must be dug to prevent the little trees from becoming waterlogged and suffocated. Indeed, on some moorland sites the water table is so high that the trees must be planted on the tops of the upturned furrows left by the huge ploughs which dig the drains. And the forester must not forget, when planting trees in areas far from civilisation, that he will eventually need roads along which to extract the timber he hopes to grow, roads that are much easier built before the trees grow up than later on.

There is one version of the high forest system, much practised in Europe where seed years are more frequent and reliable, but confined mainly to the beechwoods of southern England, which follows more closely the way in which Nature orders things. It is called the *selection system*. Little or no planting is done, the stock being maintained by natural seedlings, the result being a wood containing trees of all ages and sizes. The forester's main concern is to keep the age classes in reasonable equilibrium by removing a proportion of each age and size whenever he fells his selected main-crop trees, opening up the canopy each time just enough to allow the latest batch of seedlings to start growing. Much skill, patience and experience are required but the result is a permanent, self-perpetuating forest of great beauty which can be cropped continuously with very little change in its overall appearance.

Of course, there are many variations on the themes described, according to the situation, soil, local conditions and, indeed, the financial circumstances of the owner of the woodland. The Forestry Commission or a big landowner will be able to wait longer for a return on the investment represented by the trees than the owner of smaller woodlands who, in order to realise a quicker cash return, may plant conifers mixed in with the hardwoods or perhaps beneath them after the final thinning. Some tree species may need the protection of others in the early stages, so in the planting lines a 'nurse' species may be interspersed with the main crop. In hollows, where frost can be severe and late in the season, some lightly-crowned mature trees, such as birch, may be left to give protection to young conifers planted beneath them.

Thus does the British forester, in a variety of ways, grow timber in an infinite variety of geographical situations and in constantly changing economic circumstances; and in a land which grows trees better than almost anywhere else in Europe. But, although a forester by profession, he is usually a naturalist at heart and a true conservationist of necessity. He knows that the appearance of our landscape, although slowly but inevitably and constantly changing over the years, can suddenly, and for long periods, be transformed by what he plants or fells. He knows that his actions can replace one group of birds, animals and plants by another; and he knows that his woodlands cover the ground in the way Nature would cover it had she her way, although he is prepared to admit that her choice of species might be different from his. Nevertheless, productive woodlands and true conservation go hand in hand, for in the highly productive countryside, so necessary in our small islands, woodlands in whatever form provide vital, and in many cases the only, habitat for much of our wildlife. Many plants and some animals and birds are highly specialised and do need the protection of specially designated reserves, and these the forester will always help to establish; but very many of our birds and animals have shown themselves to be almost as adaptable as man himself and find the new woodlands perfectly acceptable and vastly better than none at all.

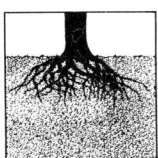

FOREST SOILS

As we shall see later, the type of soil in an area determines the species of trees found growing on it naturally, as well as those which can be planted there with success by the forester; and the composition of the soil itself is determined by the rocks from which it is derived. In general the oldest and hardest rocks are found in the north-west of Britain and the youngest and softest in the south-east. The hard rocks are of volcanic or metamorphic origin that, when broken down by the action of weather, produce for the most part soils with large mineral, or sandy, particles. Because the particles are large, these soils tend to be porous and dry out quickly. On the other hand, the younger rocks, those resulting from the sediment of volcanic rocks becoming compressed and solidified beneath prehistoric seas, contain finer particles producing more compact soils which retain moisture for much longer. Derived from one extreme of rock type to the other there is a very considerable variety of soils ranging from sandy gravels containing nothing but coarse particles to clays composed almost entirely of the finest, whilst in the middle are the loams which are made up of something like equal quantities of sand and clay. And, in addition to soils formed *in situ*, there are others which result not from the immediate bedrock but from the action of water carrying away material from its place of origin and depositing it in flat country or at river mouths, or from rock debris that was borne along by ice-age glaciers and spread over quite different rocks when the ice melted.

The basis of a soil is its mineral particles which are inert and lifeless; but it also contains organic material consisting of the decaying remains of plants and animals that have previously lived on it which is collectively called humus. In addition to this is a teeming population of minute animal and vegetable organisms whose task it is to break down this humus into a form that can be absorbed by the plants and trees. These microscopic creatures may number as many as three hundred million in one cubic foot of soil.

In forest soils the layer of humus is overlaid by a thick carpet of leaf litter in which live fungi and small animals, such as millipedes and woodlice. These assist in

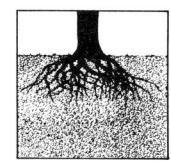

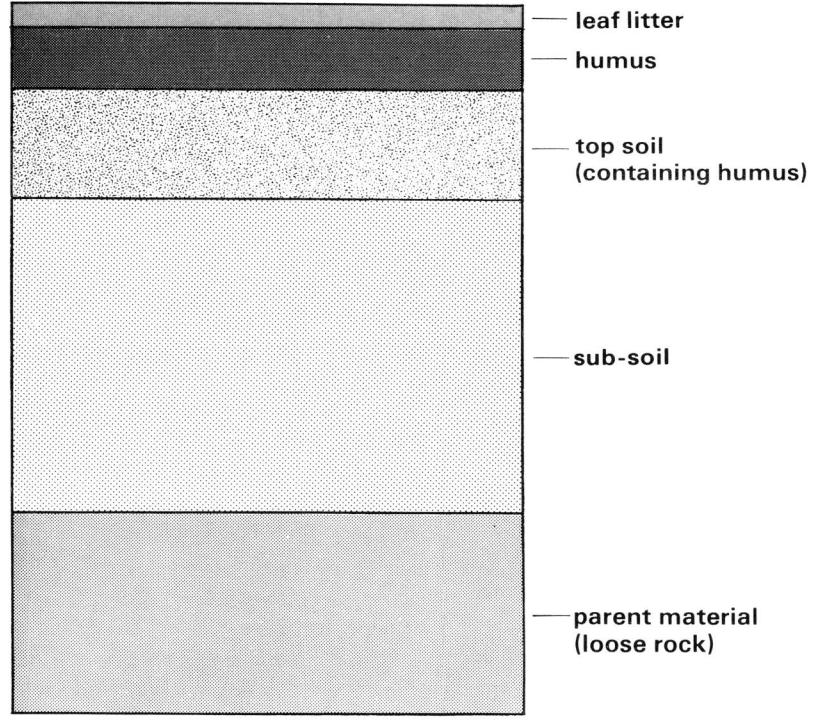

- leaf litter
- humus
- top soil (containing humus)
- sub-soil
- parent material (loose rock)

This diagram illustrates the layers found within a soil sample. The depth of the sub-soil and its drainage govern the ultimate size of the trees growing on it.

The depth of a soil formed *in situ* will depend upon the hardness of the rock which forms its basis and the amount of erosion which has taken place; but deep or shallow, it will have a number of definite layers. Beneath the leaf litter will be the soil proper—a mixture of inorganic particles and humus; then comes the sub-soil containing large and small stones as well as the smaller particles of the soil itself, but with no humus, and finally the bedrock. Upon the depth of the sub-soil and the effectiveness of the drainage of water away from it will depend the growth rate and the ultimate size of the trees, for unlike smaller plants trees send their roots to great depths. Soils which have evolved beneath trees tend to be self-fertile; there is a steady replacement of leaf and branch litter which is converted into humus, the chemical content of which is kept constant by the salts brought up from the sub-soil by the trees' roots. It is only when the tree cover is removed and the soil is exposed to the elements, or is put to another use, that the humus content

converting this litter into the much more friable humus which becomes mixed in with the upper layers of the soil by the actions of other creatures. Here earthworms are particularly important, taking down vegetable matter to a considerable depth, passing it through their bodies together with the soil, and forcing the resulting waste to the surface in the form of the familiar worm casts. It has been calculated that in the space of one year worms turn over about eleven tons of soil in each acre of ground.

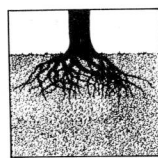

starts to fall and fertility with it.

Despite its small size, Britain contains most of the rock types found in the world and thus has a great variety of soils of which the three most important are the sandy, infertile, quick-drying types; the fine textured clays, stiff, sticky and slow to dry out; and the intermediate, fertile loams rich in humus. The colour of the soil will depend upon its chemical content; those rich in iron will vary from red to brown, those rich in humus are often very dark in colour. Soils derived from chalk and limestone are white to grey and pale yellow, for these rocks, formed from the consolidated remains of minute marine animals, are rich in calcium.

On the light, sandy, acid soils pine and birch will be the dominant woodland trees. On the neutral loams and clays oakwoods will flourish, whilst ash will thrive on the calcareous clays or marls. Beech will dominate all woodlands on the chalk and limestone except on those of magnesian origin in the northern Pennines when ash again, together with sycamore, will likely be the most numerous trees. In all cases the presence and vigour of the trees will depend upon the drainage being good. Where it is bad, sandy soils will become overlaid with thick layers of peat—the partially decomposed remains of heather, moss and grass; and over clays, marshy conditions will inhibit the growth of most trees except alder, for waterlogging of a soil drives out the air from between the particles and deprives the roots of the oxygen they need. Likewise excessive drying out will deprive both the soil animals and the roots of the trees water essential to life.

So, a good forest soil must be deep enough to provide root-hold, porous enough to absorb water but with sufficient small particles to retain it, and of such a consistency as to allow the excess of water to drain away. Given these factors, together with an equitable climate and a reasonably sheltered situation, the micro-organisms and soil animals will produce and maintain the humus content creating ground conditions which will always support trees of one species or another.

OUR NATURAL WOODLANDS

Although there are scarcely any pure examples left of our natural forests, and most of us when visiting woodlands will find ourselves in the new plantations of mixed conifers and hardwoods, the woodland types are still recognisable as such. The very conditions of soil and climate which decree the type of natural tree cover also influence the choice of species that the forester will plant. Where birch and pine have for centuries formed the natural woodland, the forester, if he wishes for economic reasons to plant other trees, will have to choose those which like essentially dry and sandy conditions. Where oakwoods predominate, trees preferring heavier soils will be chosen, and in the beechwoods trees which do not like limey soils will have to be avoided.

So, despite a huge influx of foreign trees that have greatly changed the composition and appearance of our woodlands, they are still influenced by natural conditions and the basic woodland types are still there in the background with all their attendant flora and fauna. Thus, when we explore our woods we shall, for the most part, find the same plants and animals in the new plantations as would be living in the natural woodlands. So, before we go on to describe the new trees that are such an important part of our countryside today, let us look at some of the more important natural woodland types together with their plants. Later on we shall consider the more mobile inhabitants—the birds, insects and mammals—which, because they can move from one place to another, tend to be found over a wider range of woodland types and, to some extent are less decided in their preferences.

Birchwoods

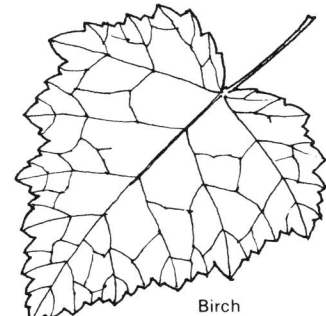

Birch

The Birch is a pioneer tree, and has been so since the Ice Age. It is hardy, seeds freely, is tolerant of many soil types and is thus one of the first trees to appear on any open ground. Only in the harsh conditions of northern Scotland and at high

altitudes elsewhere do we find permanent woodlands in which birch is the dominant tree, mostly on steep hillsides. Elsewhere, though they are widespread, for the tree is one of the commonest we have, birchwoods are transitory. They very quickly become invaded and subsequently shaded out by oak and beech on the more fertile soils and less quickly by pines on the sandier soils. Most of our birchwoods are today at one stage or another of this transition. Nevertheless, where the birch is present in any quantity the result is woodland of exceptional beauty at all seasons. In spring the trees are amongst the earliest to become tinged with green as the buds start to open and the lamb's-tail-like catkins swell, elongate and hang pendulous to shed their pollen; in summer the open crowns of delicate, oval leaves let in just enough sunlight to give the woods a bright coolness. In autumn when the leaves have gone, and throughout the winter, the fine, cascading branches take on a purplish hue which, together with the white, papery boles show up most beautifully in the reddish rays of the sinking sun.

Morrone National Nature Reserve birchwood near Braemar with juniper and ling heather beneath the birches

In the climax birchwoods of the north, where the trees themselves tend to be stunted by severe conditions, the associated plants are few. Amongst the rocks and screes in which the birch, with a few attendant rowans, miraculously gain sustenance, will be mats of moss and lichen covering the stones and often hanging in tatters from the boles and branches of the trees. Farther down the mountainside where there is more soil, albeit meagre, the trees will be of better form and shelter a considerable assortment of plants. In some places the dwarf variety of our little native conifer, the Common Juniper, will be found as bluey-green, prickly bushes curving over the rocks amidst the bright green Bilberries. Here and there will be a splash of colour from the

The scarlet, white spotted caps of the fly agaric are conspicuous when growing beneath birch trees on a gravel site

Petty Whin, a creeping gorse with golden flowers and green spines so tightly packed as to look like cushions of moss. Amongst the grasses, especially if a few pines accompany the birches, the Chickweed Wintergreen, with its running roots bearing single stems ringed with whorls of leaves, will show its large white flowers.

Most of the more transitory birchwoods are on heathland where such plants as Ling and Bell Heather, and in damper parts, Cross-leaved Heath, are very common. They seem to flourish beneath the open birch canopy, as do many other plants such as the yellow Tormentil and Heath Bedstraw, the pink Lousewort and the blue Heath Milkwort, all of them in competition with grasses such as Fine and Brown Bents, Heath Grass and Hair Grass, and often eventually shaded out by Bracken.

On the heavier soils, where the birch has a short but luxuriant reign, there is often a shrub layer of Hazel with attendant spring flowers such as Violets, Wood Anemones and even Bluebells.

The birchwood toadstools, although in very few cases exclusive to these woodlands, add colour and variety to the autumn scene, especially in a wet season. Perhaps the most striking is the Fly Agaric, poisonous and brilliant scarlet, often with white spots. Less attractive, as its name implies, is the Ugly Milkcap, yellow-brown and slimey and exuding a milk-like juice with no particular scent, unlike the small, pale lilac-coloured Coconut-scented Milkcap which has a distinctive smell. Of the edible, fungi, but not exclusive to birchwoods, is the Penny Bun with a large, brown shiny cap—a species eaten in huge quantities in Europe where it is the usual ingredient of dried mushroom soup. Many species grow on trees and of these the Birch Bracket is

common, forming thick, elastic, hoof-shaped brackets on the boles of the birches, often six inches across. Also found on birch, as well as on other trees, is the Tinder Fungus which, by adding a new layer each year to its horny, reddish-brown bracket, can grow to a great size.

Birch timber is light in colour and weight and is easily worked, but rots quickly in the open. It is used extensively for plywood, brush backs, toys and other small articles of turnery such as cotton reels. It has few outdoor uses, although the fine, wiry branches make excellent besoms.

Pinewoods

Although woods of our native tree, the Scots Pine, are fairly common throughout Britain, only those in the north of Scotland can claim to be of natural origin. In the Highlands there can still be found the remnants of natural pine forest which covered so much of that country in prehistoric times. Unlike the pine plantations and other man-made pinewoods that are widespread and which we shall discuss later, these Scottish pinewoods are fairly

The white bark and the graceful, drooping branchlets of the silver birch

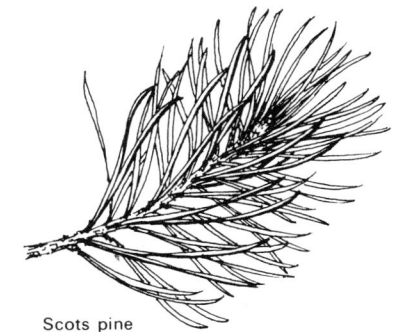

Scots pine

The bole of a fine old Scots pine at Wakehurst Place, Sussex

open. There are trees of all ages ranging from the seedlings, pushing their way through the bilberries and heather, to blue-green saplings with their orange-budded leading shoots reaching up towards the flat crowns of the old trees which, with their reddish, flaking bark give a touch of warmth to the wild scenery. Below the old pines, together with the young trees, will be Rowans and Junipers, and on the fringes some Birch. In amongst the Bilberries and Cowberries, which often grow in dense masses, there are some plants almost exclusive to pinewoods. Two are orchids: Creeping Ladies' Tresses, locally quite common with its white, unpleasant-smelling flowers on spiral spikes and its creeping, matted roots, and the much rarer Coralroot Orchid bearing creamy white flowers on a spike rising from white, coral-like roots, which subsist on rotting vegetation. There is a whole family of plants which are loosely associated with pines, namely the Wintergreens, all related to the heathers. The rarest is the One-flowered Wintergreen that has large white drooping flowers, each on a single stalk; the commonest is the Lesser Wintergreen that has many little pinkish flowers on each stalk and often strays beyond the confines of the woods. The Middle Wintergreen and the Large Wintergreen, both with large flowers and the latter with rounded leaves, are very local, particularly in Scotland, and tend to be plants of the more southerly man-made pinewoods; but the rare and beautiful little Twinflower with its double, pink flowers borne on creeping stems is confined to the pinewoods of north-east Scotland.

In the south of Britain where the pinewoods are of much more recent origin, perhaps the result of seed from old, isolated trees falling on vacant heathland or more likely artificially planted, the plant life is by no means exclusive to these particular trees. Those that are found in southern birchwoods also favour the pinewoods; heather and heath grasses, such as Wavy Hair Grass, Tormentil, Heath Bedstraw and many others all find their place except in the densest of plantations.

Like all conifer forests,

pinewoods are rich in toadstools and other fungi. Very common and destructive to the trees as the cause of root rot is the Honey Fungus which grows in yellow clusters on old stumps and travels long distances through the soil. Less damaging and very distinctive are the *Tricholomopsis rutilans*, a toadstool with a purple to reddish cap and contrasting yellow gills beneath, and the Sulphur Tuft which grows in tightly grouped clusters on old trees, stumps and decaying branches throughout the year except in the coldest months.

Scots Pine timber is strong and resinous, known in the trade severally as red deal, redwood and even yellow deal. It has many uses including structural work, pit props, telegraph poles and many kinds of joinery, of which 'knotty pine' panelling is at present a popular example.

Oakwoods

As we have seen, oakwoods once covered most of Britain and would do so again if man ceased to interfere. Thus, over much of England, Wales and the southern parts of Scotland, except in the chalk and

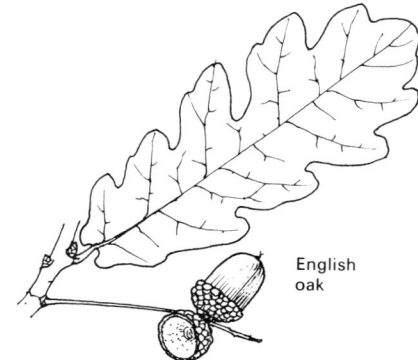

English oak

limestone areas, most of the woodlands contain a greater or lesser proportion of oaks, although in places where economic forestry is practised there will often be whole woods or compartments of exotic conifers and other tree species that thrive on the same soils as the oaks. Nevertheless, oakwoods, whether managed for timber production, semi-natural or in some measure mixed with other species, will be the type of woodland that most of us will find nearest to our homes.

In discussing the light-canopied birch and the evergreen pines we did not mention the signal change which occurs beneath the trees between spring, when the leafless canopy lets in the

strengthening sunlight in all its fullness, and summer, when the leaves cast a dense and cooling shade. In oakwoods this change is profound, for not only do the trees close their canopy as May gives way to June but the Hazel bushes, almost universally found beneath the English oaks, also come into full leaf, increasing the intensity of the shade. For this reason most of the woodland plants must come into flower before the sunlight is denied them, or at least produce enough leaves and food reserves in their roots to enable them to flower later on beneath the leafy trees. Almost before the lambs-tail catkins of the hazels have pollinated the little pink female flowers, the heart-shaped leaves of the Lesser Celandine will be followed by their shiny yellow blossoms, and at the same time the Dog's Mercury will start to cover large areas of the woodland floor with its leafy stems and small green flowers. Soon after come the Wood Anemones, raising their exquisite white star-shaped flowers in a veritable constellation around the great oak boles; whilst in amongst

Primroses are amongst the early spring flowers in oakwoods

Bluebells form blue carpets in the oak-woods before the canopy closes in early summer

the hazels and on sunny banks near the woodland edge the Primroses shine yellow from their rosettes of crumpled leaves. Finally, before the trees close up their canopy, the Bluebells form blue carpets on the woodland floor. Thus unfolds the main springtime display in our oakwoods, but many other less conspicuous plants, some confined to certain soil types, also flower before the sumer shade. Where the soils have a slight calcareous content the white flowers of the Wood Garlic will cover whole areas so that a slight crushing of the lily-like leaves fills the air with 'cooking' smells. The feathery flowers of the Wood Sanicle will emerge through their pretty, roundly-lobed leaves. Violets and Early Purple Orchids will add to the display.

As the canopy closes a new group of flowers will appear, most of them in small colonies unlike the great drifts of the spring-flowering species, although the Wood Forget-me-nots may sometimes provide large blue patches. Enjoying

the shade, the Enchanter's Nightshade raises its tiny white flowers on leafless spikes and the Herb Paris its greeny flowers above its four-leaved whorls. The flowering pyramids of Yellow Archangel and its much commoner relative, the purple Bugle, will be found amongst the tussocks of Pendulous Sedge and the rough-leaved Tufted Hair Grass. On the edges of the rides and in small clearings Willow Herb and Foxgloves will add late summer pink; and often, where the ground has been disturbed by woodland operations and

The Newland Oak in Gloucestershire, probably the oldest oak in Britain—perhaps 750 years old and quite likely 1,000. This photo was taken in the 1880s. In 1906 the girth was 43 feet; in 1954 it was 44 feet

the natural succession of things upset, the woodland floor will be carpeted with a trailing, tangled mass of Blackberries, tearing at one's clothes and making walking a burden.

On the woodland edges other trees are often to be found: Holly, the female trees bearing red berries in the autumn; Crab Apples with their pinkish blossoms in the spring and their little green apples in the autumn; and the little Goat Willows with their 'pussy' buds as the February days start to lengthen. Ivy clings to the rough-barked old oaks, whilst the climbing Honeysuckle twists itself round the saplings in iron-like, deforming bands.

Although there are no fungi exclusively found in oakwoods, the cocoa-coloured Oak Milkcap and the blackish-purple *Russula* are more likely to be found there than anywhere else. Others to be found include species which grow on stumps and on the trees themselves such as the Beefsteak Fungus which forms big liver-coloured brackets on the boles, often some nine inches across and resembling steaks when sliced.

Oak timber is hard,

beautifully grained and immensely durable in the open. Although its old uses for construction purposes and shipbuilding have almost ceased, well-grown oak timber is still in great demand and fetches very high prices for high-class joinery and for top-quality indoor panelling, staircases and furniture. For fencing posts it is still unrivalled, lasting for decades, without any signs of decay. In this age of plastics and other substitutes, oak timber more than holds its own.

Beechwoods

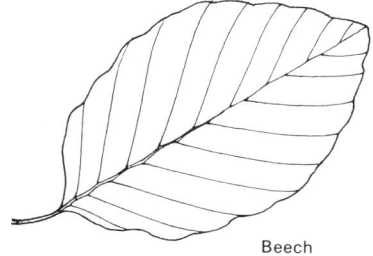

Beech

Beech was a latecomer to Britain after the ice ages and did not manage to spread much farther north than the Wash. It seems to be a much less aggressive coloniser than most of our native trees and only competes successfully

with oak on the drier, calcareous soils. Thus, the only beechwoods we have of real consequence and of natural origin are those on the chalk and limestone uplands, stretching from Hampshire north-east to the East Anglian heights, the most important areas being the Cotswolds, the Chilterns and the Downs. Here the beech, although a poor coloniser, maintains the frontiers of its empire in a firm grip. There are few woodlands more pleasant to walk in than a beechwood. In winter the tall, smooth grey boles stand in a thick carpet of dry bronze leaves; in spring the dense crowns of the trees burst into the most delicate of light greens through which the sun's rays slant in yellow beams; and in summer the intricate mosaic of the mature and leathery leaves give the coolest shade. As winter approaches again these same leaves pass through an infinite variety of red and russet hues to give beechwood country some of the most spectacular of autumn scenes. On the woodland edges the Wild Cherries blossom white in the spring, and on the escarpment slopes below the

'hangers' the leaves of the Whitebeams flash silvery in the early summer breezes; but within the deep shade of the woods few other trees can flourish. A small group of Yews or some Holly may establish themselves where an old beech has fallen, or, particularly in the south-east, some Hornbeams

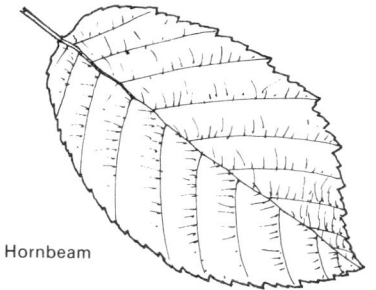

Hornbeam

may grow up with their neighbours, but there is little else and even the flowers of the woodland floor are scarce except in the clearings. There will be patches of Wood Sorrel with their delicate white, mauve-veined flowers and soft, trefoil leaves, and the Sweet Woodruff bearing small white flowers on unbranched stems with whorled leaves. Dog's Mercury, Wood Sanicle and Wild strawberries will also grow, as well as the Arum Lily with its triangular, glossy black-spotted leaves and its

purplish flowering spike, backed by a pale green hood, which dies away later leaving orange berries on the stalk. Two larger plants which will be scattered here and there are the Spurge Laurel, a small shrub with broad, leathery leaves and fragrant green flowers, and the lovely Solomon's Seal, its arching stems of broad, erect leaves hung with clusters of bell-like, whitish flowers.

In the Hangers, the beechwoods that grow on the steep escarpment slopes where the soil is thin and dry, there are even fewer plants but amongst them are two which do not need sunlight to manufacture food but which gain their sustenance from the decaying leaves and twigs upon which they are rooted and through which they poke their anaemic-looking stems. One is the Bird's Nest Orchid, about a foot tall, honey-coloured and with a rancid, sickly smell; the other the Yellow Bird's Nest, rather shorter and yellow in colour. In any clearings and on the edges of the paths Wild Strawberries will be plentiful together with some pretty grasses such as Wood Melick with its graceful

nodding heads and the tall, tufted Hairy Brome with large, drooping flower spikes.

The bare floor of the beechwoods makes the profusion of fungi easy to see. One will be our most poisonous species, the Death Cap, yellow and white spotted, with white gills. Others include the Geranium-scented *Russula*, straw-coloured in every part; the yellowish False Death Cap, which smells like new potatoes; and the Beech Tuft, which grows in little whitish groups on the beech trees themselves, like the Tinder Fungus, whose hoof-shaped, grey-topped brackets are found attached to the boles.

The white- to buff-coloured timber of the beech has long been popular for many uses. A furniture industry still flourishes round High Wycombe in the centre of the Chiltern beechwoods where until very recently the bodgers used to ply their woodland trade of turning chair legs and other products on primitive lathes. Flooring, wooden spoons, bread boards, chopping blocks are all other uses for this timber; but it is not durable in the open.

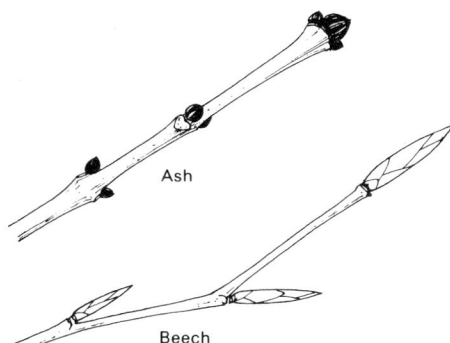

Ash

Beech

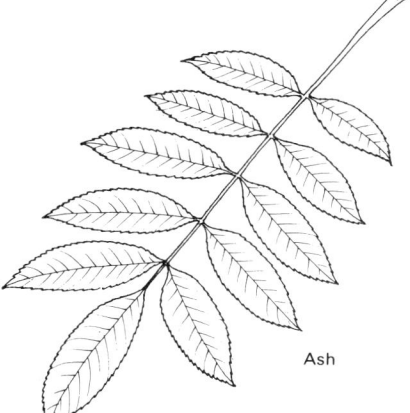

Ash

compound with little leaflets, the canopy is fairly open. The vigorous shrub layer contains Hazel, Hawthorn and Wild Roses, as well as the red-twigged Dogwood, the evergreen Wild Privet with its black berries and the white-flowered Elder beneath which the badgers so often excavate their setts. And almost exclusive to these dry, northern ashwoods is the Herb Christopher or Baneberry, a small shrub bearing feathery white flowers and later

Ashwoods

If, as we have seen, the beech is the typical tree of calcareous soils in southern Britain, then ash takes its place as the dominant tree on the limestones of the Pennines in the north. Not that the ashwoods in those parts are particularly impressive, for such rocks produce a thin, dry soil upon which ash, although thriving better than other trees, does not really grow to anything like the full stature it reaches on the rich lowland loams. Nevertheless, these northern ashwoods, despite the often stunted and gnarled appearance of the trees, are important to naturalists as habitats of an interesting if not exclusive group of plants. Because the ash leaves are

A huge old ash at Warnham Court, Sussex, shows the typical sparse branching of these trees in maturity

poisonous black berries. In some places the beautifully fragrant Lily of the Valley can occur in quite large colonies.

But these northern ashwoods, of which there is an outlier, as it were, in the Mendip Hills, are not the only places where ash trees are found; indeed, the tree is common over most of southern Britain where the soils are rich and have a calcareous content. On dry soils of this kind it is the beech that fares best, and except in damp hollows excludes the ash completely; but elsewhere, whenever the soil has just sufficient basic content to make oak slightly unhappy, the ash, if not predominating, at least holds its own and grows to very considerable dimensions. Often, those woods of this kind that contain a high proportion of ash result from an earlier time when ash coppice was maintained beneath oak standards. Neglect at some period would have been followed by a mass of ash seedlings crowding out the less numerous oak seedlings and eventually achieving some measure of dominance in maturity. In such woods many

of the plants found in the oakwoods will be present as well as such bushes as the dusty-looking Wayfaring Tree, the white-flowered Guelder Rose together with Privet and Dogwood. Perhaps, in addition to the Wood Anemones, Wood Sorrel, Dog's Mercury and Wild Garlic, especially in the more northern areas, there will be plants of the blue Giant Bellflower and little colonies of Green Hellebores with flowers like Christmas roses. Even some thistles may be present such as the Marsh Thistle, sometimes as much as six feet tall, and the Melancholy Thistle which has almost no prickles. In fact, because the ash crowns let through more light than the oaks, the range of plants beneath them is enormous.

Of fungi there are no special associations. All those common toadstools normally found in broadleaved woodland may be present. Those growing on woody debris will include the Shaggy Pholiota, its yellow caps spotted with brown flecks, the Bonnet Mycena with its humped, dirty white caps grouped in bunches, and the pleasant-smelling Oyster Mushroom; whilst King Alfred's

Cakes are often to be found as little black knobs on the ash branches.

Ash timber is yellowish-white in colour and has long been valued for its strength and elasticity. It bends well under steaming and has a great ability to withstand sudden shocks. This quality gave it a special place in the making of spokes for the wheels of carriages and carts, and nowadays it is still the best timber for all sorts of tool handles. But perhaps its most important use is in the sports industry; good, straight, quick-grown trees fetch high prices for making tennis rackets and hockey sticks. It is an excellent firewood.

Alderwoods

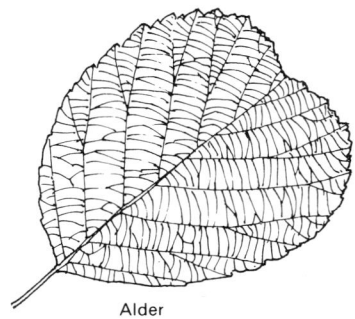

Alder

In former times, before low-lying areas were drained and cleared for agriculture,

52

alderwoods must have been widespread if limited in extent. Today such woods, or 'carrs' as they are called, are confined to the fen districts of Norfolk, although the tree is common enough along river banks and on the edges of ponds and lakes, often to the exclusion of other species but frequently in association with Ash, Willow and Wych Elm. In upland areas groups of alders are found on hillsides where springs make the soil permanently moist, as well as along the banks of becks and burns. Nowhere is this tree found far from water.

The alder carrs of the Norfolk Broads are really the only remaining associations of these trees that in any way resemble the widespread alderwoods of old. Here the alders of all ages are the dominant trees, mixed with some Ash, Goat Willows and Downy Birch, and with a wealth of shrubs and flowering plants beneath them; and because the peaty fens are saturated with lime-rich water, unlike the acid peat bogs found elsewhere, Privet, Guelder Rose and Hawthorn tend to be the commoner shrubs. Others include the Spindle Tree with its square, green stems and pink berries, and the two Buckthorns, only found growing together on these sites. The Common or Purging Buckthorn has branches which end in thorns and bears shiny, black berries; the Alder Buckthorn, which also has black berries, is unarmed and has leaves very like the alder itself. Typical of the ground plants are great grassy tumps of the tall Tussock Sedge between which will be an early summer show of yellow from Marsh Marigolds and Yellow Flags. Later the pinkish Comfrey and Marsh Valerian will appear at about the same time as the creamy-white feathery flowers of the Meadowsweet and the colourful spikes of the Purple Loosestrife. Of orchids, the flesh-coloured Early Marsh Orchid and the greeny-pink Marsh Helleborine are the more common. In late summer the lovely Grass of Parnassus will raise its white buttercup-shaped flowers on solitary stems from amidst its little ivy-shaped leaves.

Some fungi and alders seem to enjoy a mutually beneficial association; these include the reddish, saucerlike *Lactarius cyanthula* and its purple relative *Lactarius lilacinus*, but the brackets of the foxy-coloured *Polystictus radiatus* are less benevolent, growing on the rotting timber in the boles of the old trees.

Alder timber, which is a bright orange colour when first cut, but quickly fades to a light brown, was at one time much used for making clogs. It also made good charcoal, but nowadays its main but limited use is for turnery and wood pulp.

SCIENTIFIC NAMES OF PLANTS MENTIONED

Birchwoods

Common Juniper	*Juniperus communis*
Bilberry	*Vaccinium myrtillus*
Petty Whin	*Genista tinctoria*
Chickweed Wintergreen	*Trientalis europaea*
Ling	*Calluna vulgaris*
Bell Heather	*Erica cinerea*
Cross-leaved Heath	*Erica tetralix*
Tormentil	*Potentilla erecta*
Heath Bedstraw	*Galium saxatile*
Lousewort	*Pedicularis sylvatica*
Heath Milkwort	*Polygala serpyllifolia*
Fine Bent	*Agrostis tenuis*
Brown Bent	*Agrostis canina*
Heath Grass	*Sieglingia decumbens*
Hair Grass	*Deschampsia caespitosa*
Bracken	*Pteridium aquilinum*
Hazel	*Corylus avellana*
Wood Anemone	*Anemone nemorosa*
Bluebell	*Endymion non-scriptus*
Fly Agaric	*Amanita muscaria*
Ugly Milkcap	*Laccaria turpis*
Coconut-scented Milkcap	*Laccaria glyciosmus*
Penny Bun	*Boletus edulis*
Birch Bracket	*Polyporus betulinus*
Tinder Fungus	*Fomes fomentarius*

Pinewoods

Cowberry	*Vaccinium vitis-idaea*
Creeping Ladies' Tresses	*Goodyera repens*
Coralroot Orchid	*Corallorhiza trifida*
One-flowered Wintergreen	*Moneses uniflora*
Lesser Wintergreen	*Pyrola minor*
Medium Wintergreen	*Pyrola media*
Twinflower	*Linnaea borelais*
Wavy Hair Grass	*Deschampsia flexuosa*
Honey Fungus	*Armillaria mellea*
Sulphur Tuft	*Hypholoma fasciculare*

Oakwoods

Lesser Celandine	*Ranunculus ficaria*
Dog's Mercury	*Mercurialis perennis*
Wood Anemone	*Anemone nemorosa*
Primrose	*Primula vulgaris*
Wood Garlic	*Allium ursinum*
Early Purple Orchid	*Orchis mascula*
Wood Forget-me-not	*Myosotis sylvatica*
Enchanter's Nightshade	*Circaea lutetiana*

Herb Paris	Paris quadrifolia
Yellow Archangel	Galeobdolon luteum
Bugle	Ajuga reptans
Pendulous Sedge	Carex pendula
Tufted Hair Grass	Deschampsia caespitosa
Willow Herb	Chamaenerion angustifolium
Foxglove	Digitalis purpurea
Blackberry	Rubus fruticosus
Holly	Ilex aquifolium
Crab Apple	Malus sylvestris
Goat Willow	Salix caprea
Ivy	Hedera helix
Honeysuckle	Lonicera periclymenum
Oak Milkcap	Laccaria quietus
Beefsteak Fungus	Fistulina hepatica

Beechwoods

Wild Cherry	Prunus avium
Whitebeam	Sorbus aria
Yew	Taxus baccata
Hornbeam	Carpinus betulus
Wood Sorrel	Oxalis acetosella
Sweet Woodruff	Galium odoratum
Wood Sanicle	Sanicula europaea
Wild Strawberry	Fragaria vesca
Arum Lily	Arum maculatum
Spurge Laurel	Daphne laureola
Solomon's Seal	Polygonatum multiflorum
Bird's Nest Orchid	Neottia nidus-avis
Yellow Bird's Nest	Monotropa hypopytis
Wood Melick	Melica uniflora
Hairy Brome	Bromus ramosus
Death Cap	Amanita phalloides
Tinder Fungus	Fomes fomentarius

Ashwoods

Hawthorn	Crataegus monogyna
Dogwood	Thelycrania sanguinea
Wild Rose	Rosa canina
Privet	Ligustrum vulgare
Elder	Sambucus nigra
Herb Christopher	Actaea spicata
Lily of the Valley	Convallaria majalis
Wayfaring Tree	Viburnum lantana
Guelder Rose	Viburnum opulus
Giant Bellflower	Campanula latifolia
Green Hellebore	Helleborus viridus
Marsh Thistle	Carduus palustre
Melancholy Thistle	Carduus heterophyllum
Shaggy Pholiota	Pholiota squarrosa
Bonnet Mycena	Mycena galericulata
Oyster Mushroom	Pleurotus ostreatus
King Alfred's Cakes	Daldinia concentrica

Alderwoods

Common Buckthorn	Rhamnus cathartica
Alder Buckthorn	Frangula alnus
Tussock Sedge	Carex paniculata
Marsh Marigold	Caltha palustris
Yellow Flag	Iris pseudacorus
Comfrey	Symphytum officinale
Marsh Valerian	Valeriana dioica
Meadowsweet	Filipendula vulgaris
Purple Loosestrife	Lythrum salicaria
Early Marsh Orchid	Dactylorchis incarnata
Marsh Helleborine	Epipactis palustris
Grass of Parnassus	Parnassia palustris

INTRODUCED FOREST TREES

As we have seen, the severance of Britain from the Continent left us without several forest trees found elsewhere in Europe, and these were subsequently introduced from Roman times onwards. Much later still, when adventurers explored the temperate world, other trees were found—particularly in north-west America—which now have an important place in our forests and woodlands.

The Sycamore

Of the European trees the Sycamore or Great Maple with its great, scaly-barked bole, bright green winter buds, its three-lobed leaves and dangling tresses of 'keys', has been outstandingly successful. No other tree introduced by man has, with so little help from him, spread so widely in

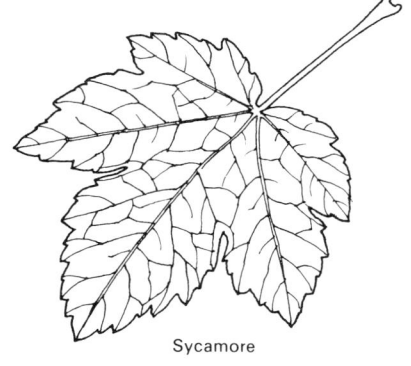

Sycamore

Britain. It has become naturalised in practically every part of the country and it is the only introduced tree which increases in numbers of its own accord; indeed, if man ceased to inhabit these islands, it would undoubtedly compete successfully with our native trees. The exact limits of its natural range are difficult to define as the tree has for centuries been planted outside

its original home, which certainly includes the Alps, the Pyrenees and the Carpathians. Likewise, the date of its introduction into Britain is uncertain; possibly the Romans brought it with them, although there is no mention of its being planted here until Gerard wrote of it in 1597. But whenever it was first planted, it has never looked back and it is now almost everywhere a constituent, often unwelcome, of most woodland types. It fares best on the heavy soils and thus poses a considerable threat to the oaks. Seeding in profusion every year, unlike the much less prolific oaks, it colonises any clearings or felled areas and, unless removed by forest operations, quickly forms pure stands of saplings in which oak seedlings stand no chance. As the timber is hard,

are caused by a fungus called Tar Spot and it is interesting to note that trees growing in or near towns, where there is air pollution from factories, do not suffer from this fungus.

The Sweet Chestnut

A 200-year-old sycamore now in the centre of a school playground in Tring, Herfordshire

even-grained and white in colour it is valuable for veneering, especially when it comes from trees with a rare and curious curly grain. Sycamore is sometimes grown in plantations, especially in the north, although for the most part it is tolerated as a forest tree only as isolated individuals or in small groups in plantations of other species. But it has its uses beyond the economic forestry sphere. Its hardiness and its ability to cope with constant winds make it an ideal tree for shelterbelts and windbreaks in northern areas, where it is often found guarding hill farmsteads; and the massive spread of crown it develops when grown in the open makes it a fine tree for park and hedgerow planting.

No matter what woodlands you visit, you are almost sure to find some sycamores growing in it; and on the leaves in summer you will most likely find black spots. These

The Sweet Chestnut, so called to distinguish it from the beautiful flowering Horse Chestnut which produces inedible 'conkers', is another tree that was probably introduced by the Romans. A native of southern Europe, western Asia and North Africa, it is less hardy than the sycamore and in Britain does not bear the large *marrons*, but much smaller nuts which are only occasionally fertile and not particularly good to eat. Nevertheless, it does reproduce itself in good seed years in the south of England

Sweet chestnut

An old sweet chestnut at Chatsworth House, Derbyshire

where it has long been grown especially as coppice to provide, amongst other things, poles for the hopfields of Kent. Chestnut woodland as such is rare today and small in extent but there are still many old trees to be found growing in the oakwoods, for they have the same soil preferences.

Sweet chestnut coppice grown in Kent for hop poles

Some of these are fine, upright trees; their rough, grooved bark, spiralling upwards round the trunks, their large, oblong tooth-edged leaves which turn yellow in the autumn, and the nuts in their spiny husks, distinguish them from the oaks to which they bear some superficial resemblance. They also vie with the oaks for longevity. One tree at Tortworth in Gloucestershire was described by John Evelyn as a giant in 1706. Still there today, albeit a somewhat twisted wreck, it has survived since the beginning of the fourteenth century, if not well before.

The chestnut produces a good and durable timber, very much like that of the oak but without the beautiful figuring of the latter when cut on the quarter. It was used for constructional purposes and for barrel making, and as it cleaves well and easily, it was, and to some extent still is, popular for fencing posts and palings.

The Larches

Of the European conifers, the European Larch was the first to be planted in Britain on a forest scale. The tree, a native

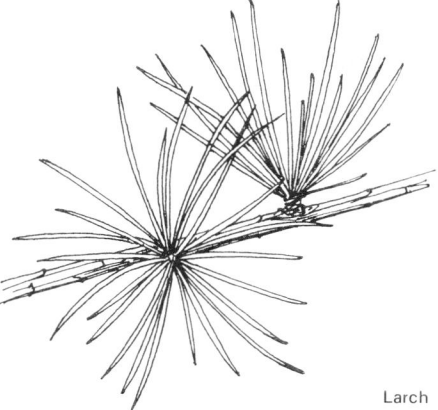

Larch

of the eastern Alps and essentially a mountain species, was first introduced around 1764 when the first Duke of Atholl planted ten thousand acres of larch. The success of this venture and the excellent timber resulting from it, encouraged other landowners and larchwoods became a major feature of the Scottish landscape, later spreading to the rest of Britain; and few will deny today that this most elegant of trees has greatly added to the beauty of our countryside. There are few more delicate or more welcome greens than the rosettes of larch needles in early spring, often interspersed with the pink female flowers; and the butter-yellow of the trees in autumn before the leaves fall (for the

A European larch plantation at Huntley, Gloucestershire. The light canopy allows a profuse growth of ground flora including bracken and other plants

larch is a rare phenomenon—a deciduous conifer) contrasts most agreeably with the more sombre and permanent greens of the evergreen conifers.

The larch cannot tolerate very dry or very chalky soils and is thus most at home on the richer soils where our native oaks and ash grow. Here pure larch plantations are common, differing from other coniferous woods in the amount of sunlight that filters through the open, feathery canopy enabling the growth of a considerable ground flora, particularly grasses. Sometimes larches are planted as 'nurses' for hardwood crops and you may find quite tall trees growing over much smaller oaks. After twenty years or so these larches will be removed, their poles being readily saleable for rustic work and for fencing, and the oaks will be left to grow on to maturity after the benefit of a sheltered childhood. Sometimes, too, a wood of mature larches, anything from sixty to a hundred years old, will be under-planted with shade-bearing trees, such as beech or hemlocks, some years before it is felled, to provide a continuity of tree cover. But larch woodlands, be they pure or mixed, have a special charm of their own, for they are never dark and dreary, but are bright and colourful at all times of the year.

Frequently, trees bred in one habitat will fail when planted in another, even though it may be more benign. This is especially so with larch, which is essentially an alpine tree. In the early days after its introduction, seedlings from the mountain trees were planted in lowland Britain and as they grew became very prone to attack from fungal and bacterial diseases. This fault, the cause of which was unrecognised at the time, resulted in the Japanese Larch gaining rapidly in favour after its introduction in 1861, and the tree is still planted on a large scale. Coming from a somewhat similar maritime climate to our own, it grows well in Britain and is thus more resistant to disease than the European species; it is also more tolerant of base rich soils. When in leaf the two species closely resemble one another, but in the winter the pink twigs of the Japanese are noticeably

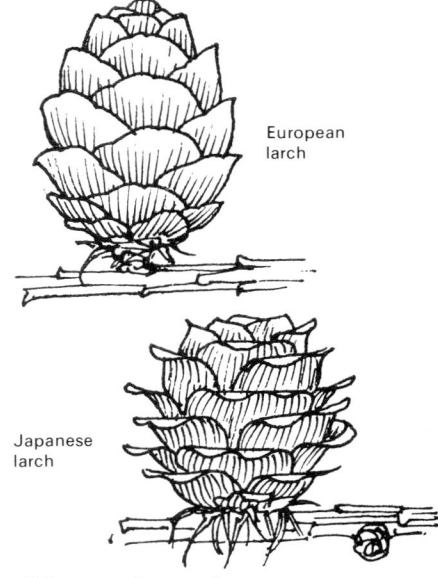

European larch

Japanese larch

different from the straw-coloured ones of the European, and the cones of the former have reflexed scales and look like little, brown dried-up roses. A hybrid between the two species, first noticed at Dunkeld, Scotland, in 1897, seems to combine the hardiness of one parent with the disease resistance of the other and is now finding favour with foresters.

Larch timber, reddish-brown in colour and both strong and durable, is highly valued for constructional purposes, railway sleepers, boat building and for

gates and fences. Large trees are particularly valuable for making boat 'skins'—the wooden shells which cover the internal framework of boats. The poles of small trees are much in demand for rustic work in gardens, and medium-sized trees, when sawn into thin planks, provide the inter-woven fences marketed under a number of trade names including 'Larchlap'. Of all the coniferous timber grown in Britain, that of the larches, with its rusty coloured, attractive grain, is the most popular and widely used.

The Spruces

Norway spruce

Much more widely planted than the larches are the spruces: evergreen conifers of formal pyramidal shape, with prickly needles growing either side of the twigs like the teeth of a comb. The Norway Spruce was a pre-glacial native of Britain, but after the Ice Age managed only to re-establish itself in the mountains of central Europe, and was reintroduced to Britain around the year 1500. Like the European larch, it is a mountain species, hardy and tolerant of many soil conditions. It did not attract much attention from foresters until the latter part of the nineteenth century since when, and especially after the founding of the Forestry Commission in 1919, it has been very widely planted. Spruce woods are found on a wide variety of sites and soils except those which are very acid and dry out quickly and those with a high basic content. Perhaps they are found more often in upland areas where broadleaved trees are less happy, although care must be taken to avoid, if possible, situations which habitually bear the brunt of high winds, for spruce is very shallow-rooted and is easily

A huge Sitka spruce felled across Highway 99, Northern California, by a hurricane in 1962. The diameter of the trunk, even where the men are standing, was nearly 6 feet

blown over. For this reason it is often planted in relatively small blocks, sheltered by more wind-firm species. Our Christmas trees are Norway spruce and plantations are often grown specially for this market, although nowadays, with the public less concerned to buy trees with their roots still attached, this Yuletide decoration is often just the top section of a larger tree removed in thinning operations. Most

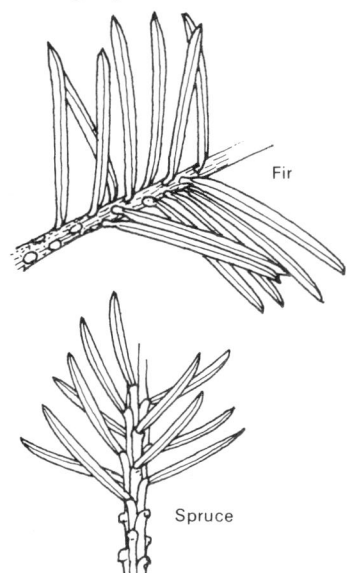

people will thus be familiar with the little green needles of this spruce, but may not have noticed that when they fall

they leave little woody pegs on the twigs, making them very rough to the touch. This is a sure identifying feature of all spruces.

The other species of spruce which now forms huge areas of forest in the west and the north of upland Britain is the Sitka Spruce—a giant tree of coastal British Columbia and Alaska, introduced in 1831, which showed by the turn of the century an ability to grow very rapidly on exposed and difficult sites in Britain. Like the

Japanese larch, it comes from a climate much more like our own than that of central Europe and it is extremely happy in the high rainfall areas of western Britain. In the last thirty years more Sitka spruce has been planted here than any other species and vast areas now carry forests of this tree, although its susceptibility to windthrow on shallow, peaty soils has now shown these plantings to have been a mistake in some places. Admittedly, in their young

A Sitka spruce plantation in Quantock Forest, Somerset

stages, plantations of this prickly tree are unattractive and impenetrable, but as the trees grow up and are thinned out, their bluey-green foliage, some in sunshine, some in shade on undulating valley slopes, give a new and pleasing variety to the moorland scene. It is the powder-blue colouring of the undersides of its larger, more prickly needles which distinguish the Sitka from the Norway spruce, as well as the much smaller cones that hang down from the upper branches; those of the Norway are as much as six inches long and the Sitka's rarely more than half that length.

These 50-year-old Sitka spruce at Ballykelly, Ulster, show the typical scaly bark

Twenty-year-old Norway spruce at Redleaf, Kent

Spruce timber, known as white deal or whitewood, is creamy-white in colour and has a wide variety of indoor uses ranging from flooring, furniture and box-making—being particularly good at holding nails—to pulp for paper-making, the latter use being the chief market for plantations in this country. The light, strong timber of Sitka spruce was in great demand for aeroplane construction in the last war.

The Douglas Fir

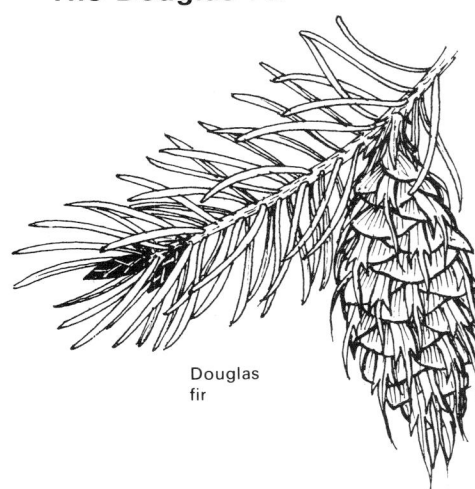

Douglas fir

Another native of north-west America is the Douglas Fir, one of the world's most remarkable trees. It forms vast forests from British Columbia south to

A group of 120-year-old Douglas firs at Bolderwood, New Forest

California, and individual trees may exceed three hundred feet in height and forty feet in girth. Here again we have a tree well suited to our climate, and ever since its introduction in 1827 it has enjoyed the reputation of being an excellent timber tree, as well as one of exceptional size and beauty. Superficially not unlike the spruces to look at from afar, it differs in having much softer needles and very characteristic, pointed buds, rather like those of the beech. The cones, too, differ in having three-pronged bracts protruding beyond the scales.

Douglas firs like well-drained soils which are not too heavy or too base-rich and which are kept moist by a reasonably high rainfall. Thus they are mostly planted in oak country and usually on valley slopes where drainage is good and where, perhaps, old oak coppice has been removed. A mature plantation of these trees is an inspiring sight; the huge, corky-barked boles are often bare of branches for fifty feet and more, supporting a light green canopy like the roof of some vast building.

The reddish timber of Douglas fir is first rate and is

greatly prized for constructional purposes and for joinery. Because of the large sizes available, it is excellent for veneering and for plywood, the latter being used extensively for the walls of temporary buildings and for hoardings round building sites in towns. The smaller timber is used for fencing and pit props.

The Pines

In addition to our native Scots Pines, two other pines, one from Europe and one from north-west America, are planted in Britain as forest trees and form considerable woodlands in certain parts of the country. The most widely planted is the Corsican Pine—a native of that island, south Italy and Sicily—which was introduced in 1759. It differs from the Scots pine in having an altogether darker aspect and needles which are twice as long and grey-green in colour. The bark, too, instead of being orange is pale grey. The chief attraction of Corsican pine to foresters is its ability to put on timber twice as fast as the Scots in similar conditions of soil and rainfall, and in addition it will thrive on base-rich, even

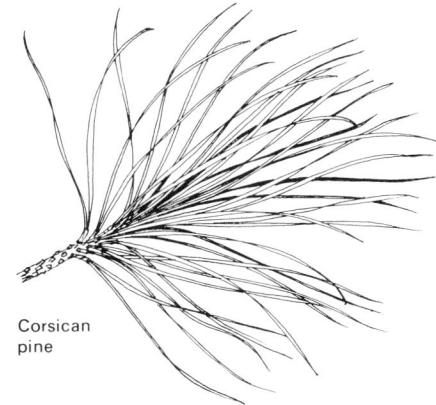

Corsican pine

Lodgepole pine

chalky, soils and will put up with occasional periods of drought. It also has a great resistance to salty winds from off the sea and will grow well even when planted in almost pure sand in coastal regions. In many parts of the country on the lighter soils, where rainfall is low and where Scots pine plantations have long been grown, replanting with Corsican pine is seen as a good way of increasing the

timber yield. In Thetford Forest, Norfolk, for instance, extensive areas have been planted with this species, replacing the original Scots pine when it reached maturity.

The timber is not so strong as that of the Scots and is thus less popular with the merchants; nevertheless, it is a good general-purpose timber grown quickly on sites where few other trees would do half so well.

Another variety of this species, known as the Austrian Pine, and native of south-east Europe, has dark green shorter needles and is almost black-looking from afar. Its much larger side branches mean that it is little used for forest planting. But, being very hardy and wind-resistant, it is often planted for shelter, particularly in coastal areas, and is frequently seen in parks and suburban gardens.

The second exotic pine which is planted extensively as a forest tree is the Lodgepole Pine, so called because the Red Indians used to support their lodges or wigwams on the stout poles of these trees. It is a native of north-west America and was introduced to Britain

in 1855. The coastal race, subsequently found to be the most suitable for planting here, is yet another example of a north-west American tree finding our climate much to its liking. Since the last war many thousand acres of windswept, peaty moorland have been planted up with it, and although it is a slow-grower by American standards, it is providing valuable tree cover and shelter in what were bleak places. It produces a modicum of good timber closely resembling that of Scots pine and in conditions in which the latter tree would not flourish. The Lodgepole pine has short, yellowish-green needles, thickly covering the somewhat contorted shoots and cones which persist on the stems for many years.

The Firs

The firs resemble the spruces superficially but have blunter, wider needles which, when they fall, do not leave wooden pegs behind on the twigs but take their stalks with them, leaving round scars. Their cones, too, instead of hanging down like those of the spruces,

Corsican pine, 98 years old, at Knightswood, New Forest

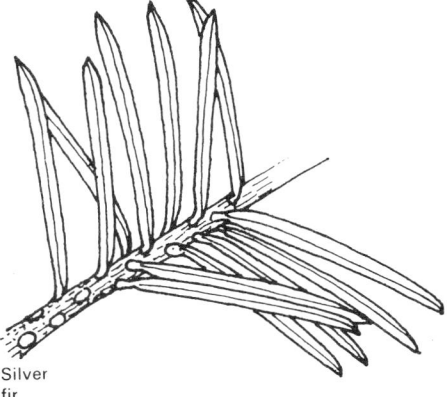

Silver
fir

stand upright on the branches
like candles on a Christmas
tree.

The European Silver Fir
failed to reach Britain before
the land bridge was severed
and was only introduced in
1603. Being a native of the
mountains of central and
south-east Europe, it is a tree
thriving in a continental climate
which may account for its
decreasing resistance to a small
leaf-sucking insect which, in
about the year 1900, started to
decimate plantations in Britain.
Since then it has rarely been
planted although up and down
the country are some very fine
specimen Silver Firs, one of
which, in Scotland, at 181 feet
in height, is the tallest tree in
Britain.

A young lodgepole pine plantation in Cannock Chase, Staffordshire

To replace this European tree, foresters turned to the Giant Fir, introduced in 1832 from north-west America, where it grows to huge dimensions and fine symmetry of form, often exceeding three hundred feet in height. Its needles are much longer and brighter green than those of the Silver Fir, and are more evenly arranged either side of the twigs, like a broad-toothed comb. The smooth bark of young trees is covered with blisters containing pleasant-smelling resin. The tree seems to favour the better soils and is often planted in mixture with larch or ash in areas where old oak coppice is being converted to a more productive use, for this fir grows at a phenomenal rate and puts on large volumes of good, white timber in a very short time.

Also introduced from north-west America, in 1830, was the Noble Fir, which has dark, grey-green needles arranged in a much more haphazard fashion on the twigs, pointing forwards, sideways and even upwards; but the most striking feature of this tree is the immense cones which stand brown, cylindrical and a good

A 150-year-old European silver fir at Whitfield Hall, Northumberland, which tops 117 feet and girths over 11 feet

six inches long, crowded and often weighing down the upper branches. Although it seems to be hardier and less easily damaged by wind than the Giant Fir, its excessive cone production and its strange tendency to die back in middle age for no apparent reason make it a less popular tree with foresters. Nevertheless, small plantations of it are quite common and there are some very fine individual specimens in many parts of the country.

There are several other trees, all from north-west America, which are finding increasing favour with foresters. The **Western Hemlock,** introduced in 1851, is one which, because of its extreme tolerance of shade conditions, is much planted as an under-crop to maturing broadleaved trees. Its very short needles, arranged rather like the firs, and its tiny cones, distinguish this tree as does, in its early years, the elegant, drooping leading shoot. The tree seeds freely in Britain and seedlings beneath the parent trees often grow as thickly as mustard and cress. The light-coloured timber is good for general purposes and for pulping.

The smooth-barked giant firs are easily distinguished from the rough-barked Douglas firs in this mixed plantation in Kyloe Wood, Northumberland

69

The massive bole of this noble fir at Stourhead, Wiltshire, measures over 11 feet in circumference

The drooping, feathery fronds of this western hemlock are accentuated by a sprinkling of snow

The **Western Red Cedar,**
introduced two years later, has
scaly leaves like the cypress
and produces the well-known,
naturally rot-proof, reddish
timber which is much in
demand for many outdoor uses
such as home extensions,
greenhouses, roof shingles and
rugger goal posts. Like the
hemlock it stands shade well
and, on good soils, is often
planted in mixture with
hardwoods and other conifers.

Very similar in appearance,
but with round as opposed to
urn-shaped cones, is the

Red
cedar

Cypress

Lawson Cypress, introduced
in 1854. Although not a forest
tree of any great importance in
Britain, it is frequently planted
along the edges of woodland
where its feathery foliage is not
only good to look at but, being
persistent down to the ground,
provides excellent shelter. This
tree is remarkable for the
number of varieties it has
produced: blue, golden,

Open-grown western red cedars at the National Pinetum, Bedgebury, Kent, are almost perfect cones

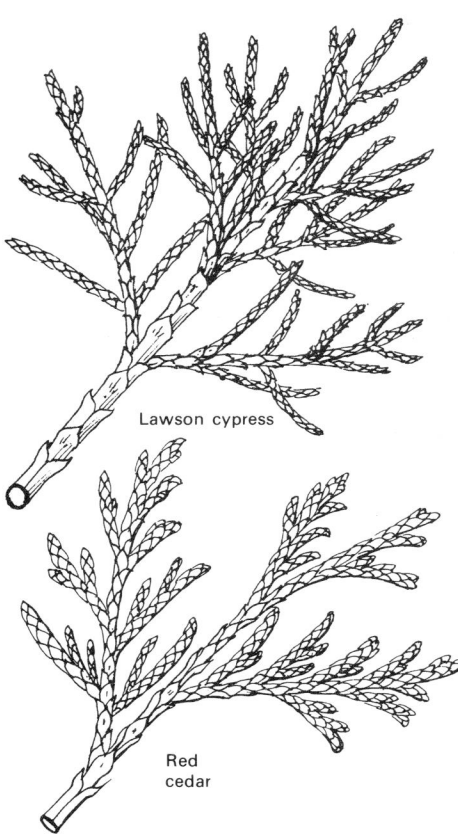

Lawson cypress

Red cedar

spreading, upright and dwarf—
in one form or another it finds
a place in nearly every garden.
The foliage of cypress and of
red cedar are commonly used
in the making of wreaths.

The shapes, colours and textures of the
Lawson cypresses in Cypress Valley at
the National Pinetum, Bedgebury, Kent,
are as varied as they are beautiful

SCIENTIFIC NAMES OF TREES MENTIONED

Sycamore
   Acer pseudoplatanus
Sweet Chestnut
   Castanea sativa
European Larch
   Larix decidua
Japanese Larch
   Larix kaempferi
Norway Spruce
   Picea abies
Sitka Spruce
   Picea sitchensis
Douglas Fir
   Pseudotsuga menziesii
Corsican Pine
   Pinus nigra var. *maritima*
Austrian Pine
   Pinus nigra var. *nigra*
Lodgepole Pine
   Pinus contorta
European Silver Fir
   Abies alba
Giant Fir
   Abies grandis
Noble Fir
   Abies procera
Western Hemlock
   Tsuga heterophylla
Western Red Cedar
   Thuya plicata
Lawson Cypress
   Chamaecyparis lawsoniana

WOODLAND INSECTS

Of the animal kingdom, insects form by far the greatest tribe, and amongst them the variety of their shapes and size, the complexity of their life cycles and the diversity of their feeding habits are remarkable in the extreme. But they are all invertebrates: that is, they have no skeleton, but an external frame; and they have no lungs but breathe through external pores; and as their body temperature is that of the surrounding air, they are obliged to lie dormant during the winter months. Compared with the higher forms of life, such as birds and mammals, they are thus at a considerable disadvantage, but they well make up for this by their incredible powers of rapid reproduction, and by the very diversities mentioned above; for an insect can have as many as

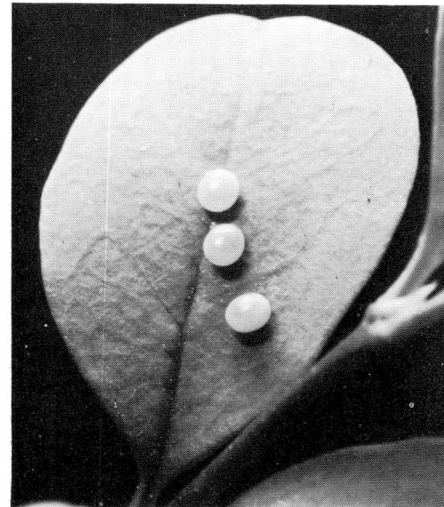

The eggs of a privet hawk moth on the leaves of a privet

four distinct stages of life in each of which it differs totally in appearance. A tiny round egg attached to a leaf will become a big, hairy caterpillar munching its way through the plant on which it was born

before becoming static again as a horny pupa or chrysalis from which, in due course, it will emerge as a brightly coloured butterfly. Such is the chain of events in the existence of most insects, although some of them may leave out one or more of the stages, and in by no means all of them is the end-result so attractive as in the butterflies and moths. But each one and each stage has its part to play in the complex arrangements of life as a whole; some provide food for other creatures, others increase the fertility of the soil by helping to break down the humus, yet others are hosts to other insects or prey upon the more prolific and keep their numbers in check. Their interdependence upon each other and the dependence of other creatures upon them is fascinating and far-reaching.

Caterpillars of the cinnabar moth feeding on ragwort

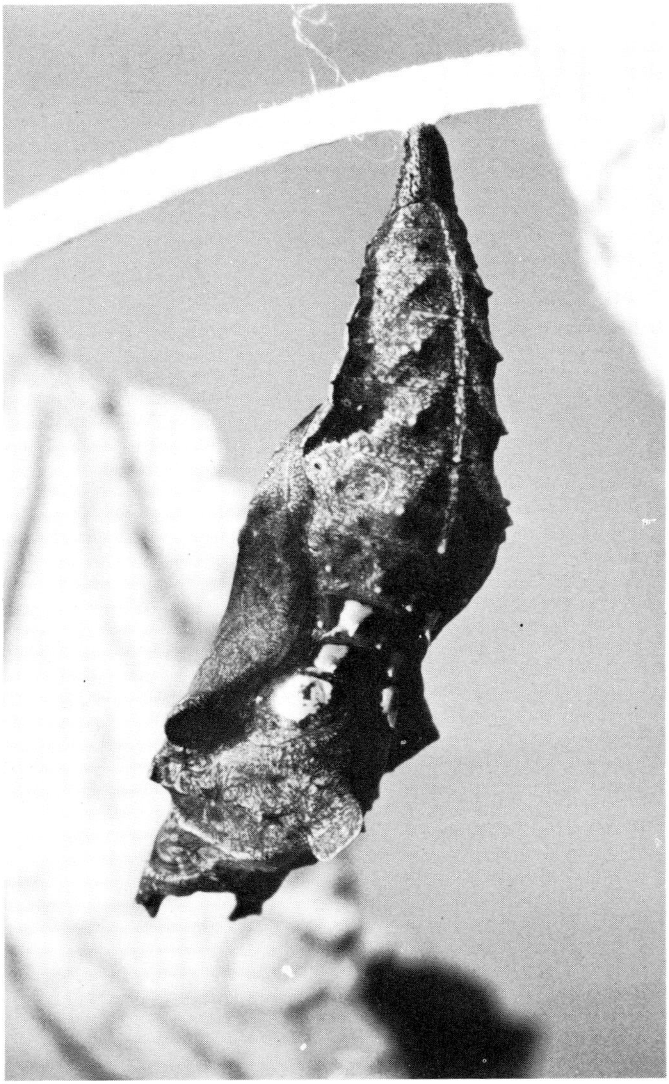

A butterfly pupa

Woodlands are exceptionally rich in insect life, for within them there is more food and more shelter than anywhere else. Yet, in the natural order of things, neither the myriad of tiny insects nor the great trees gains the upper hand; a singular balance is struck. Many insects feed upon the living tree, but many others prey upon these leaf-eaters and restore the balance. Some eat only dead wood or feed upon the leaf-litter, boosting soil fertility; others are vital to some trees in carrying pollen from one flower to another. So, unless Nature interferes drastically by such aberrations as floods, tempests or droughts, or man upsets the balance by planting too many of the same species of tree over too large an area, giving one particular insect an unusual advantage, the equilibrium is maintained.

So numerous are the woodland insects that we can mention only a few from some of the many types which, because of their numbers, their beauty or the damage they do, are likely to be noticed. But, as everyone who visits woods in summer knows, the cool space beneath the trees is alive with these little creatures; caterpillars hang suspended from the branches on silken threads, flies buzz helplessly in the grip of spiders' webs, butterflies flit across the clearings, ants cross the paths in endless processions, and from the great tree canopy there is the constant hum of countless tiny wings.

The insects which live amongst and eat the leaves of trees are chiefly the caterpillar stages of moths and butterflies. Very numerous and often damaging is the Green Oak Roller Moth which lays its eggs on the young twigs of the oak during the summer, the little green caterpillars not appearing until the following spring when they emerge to feed upon the leaves, which they roll up to protect themselves during pupation. The moths themselves are small and greenish and, being nocturnal, are seldom seen. There are two other common moths whose caterpillars feed on oak, beech and other forest trees, sometimes causing great damage: the Mottled Umber and the Winter Moth. Both drop to the ground to pupate, the flightless female moths appearing in late autumn to crawl up the trees and lay their eggs in crevices in the bark and in lichen on the boles and branches. Feeding on oak, birch and elm, but rarely in epidemic numbers, are the caterpillars of two handsome black-and-white moths, the Oak Beauty and the Peppered Moth, the latter sometimes adding beech and fruit trees to its menu, as well as being partial to birch leaves. The green caterpillar, with broad white lines along its back, seen munching the needles of Scots pine is that of the Pine Beauty, a pretty little russet-coloured moth which emerges in the spring at the flowering time of the goat willows and can be seen flying amongst the yellow flowers of an evening. In early winter in most woodlands, when there are not many other insects about, the little brown November Moths are frequently disturbed in the shrubs as one walks along; the green caterpillars feed on oak, elm, birch and many other trees. Much preferring beechwoods is the Lobster Moth, a species with a truly remarkable-looking caterpillar, grotesquely horny with a tail which it bends back

over its head in aggressive display when disturbed whilst feeding on the beech leaves. The large moth itself is grey-brown and is in no way extraordinary. One of the largest moths is the Goat Moth, with a wingspan of more than three inches; the caterpillars which take three to four years to reach maturity, feed on the solid timber of ash, elm and willow; but one could go on indefinitely, for there are more than 130 species of moths whose caterpillars feed on oak leaves alone, let alone the many hundreds which feed on other trees and smaller plants.

Oddly enough the only butterfly whose caterpillar feeds on oak leaves is the Purple Hairstreak, a little blackish-brown butterfly with iridescent purple markings on its upper wings, which flits about the crowns of the trees in July. But the caterpillars of yellow-spotted, brownish Speckled Wood feed on woodland grasses and the insect is mostly seen flying beneath the trees where the sun's rays penetrate in golden shafts. One of the earliest and most common butterflies to be seen in woodland clearings on base-

Lobster moth caterpillar on a beech twig

rich soils—for their food plants are the two buckthorns—is the uniformly bright yellow Brimstone; and later in the spring the Red Admiral, with vivid contrasting black and scarlet colours, can be seen along the rides searching for young nettles in which to lay its eggs. At about the same time the fulvous, black-spotted Silver-washed Fritillary will lay its eggs on the tree trunks from where the velvety-black caterpillars will fall in search of woodland violets on which they feed. As June gives way to July that most graceful flier, the black-and-white White Admiral, will skim through the woodland glades.

In the summer a number of different curious swellings and blemishes on oak leaves and twigs may be noticed. They are all caused by the egg-laying activities of a group of little insects called Gall Wasps. The well-known Oak Apples are not fruits but deformities of the buds into the bases of which the female gall wasp has laid her eggs; cherry galls, the globular reddish objects attached to the undersides of the leaves, result from eggs being laid in the leaf veins, and

Oak spangle galls on the underside of an oak leaf

the little round golden discs found in large numbers on the undersides of oak leaves are called Spangle Galls and also result from the egg-laying activities of a gall wasp. Many other deformities found on the leaves and twigs of other trees are also caused by insects, although virus attacks can do the same sort of thing.

In pinewoods one sometimes

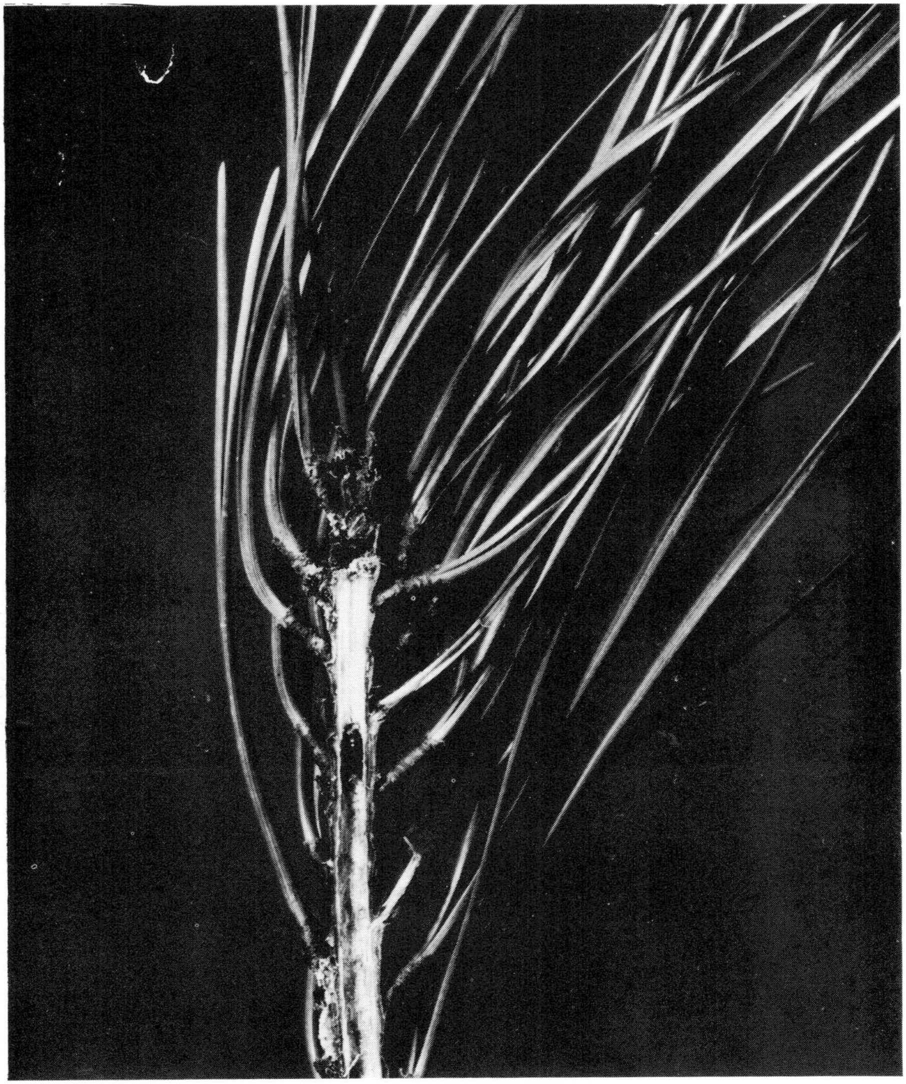

sees the needles on whole shoots eaten off right down to the stem. This damage is caused by the pale green caterpillars of the Pine Sawfly, a fat bluebottle-like insect with a saw-like egg-laying tube with which it cuts slits in the needles into which it inserts its eggs. In other pine plantations the shoots themselves may be mis-shaped and stunted; the culprit here will be the Pine-shoot Beetle which lays its eggs on the trunks, preferably of felled trees, after cutting tunnels beneath the bark. The young, fully formed beetles emerge through tiny holes and immediately attack the leading shoots of the trees, themselves cutting tunnels in which they feed. Even more damage can be done to the leading shoots of pines by the Pine Weevil, a long-snouted beetle which feeds on the thin bark, causing the death of the whole shoot above the damaged portion; and it is another beetle which feeds on elms, carrying the deadly Dutch Elm Disease fungus from one tree to another.

On the ground amongst the leaf-litter is a myriad of tiny and not so tiny insects, most of

Pineshoot beetles feeding on the shoot of a pine

The central elm in this group has been killed by Dutch elm disease and those on the right are badly affected

them doing an excellent job helping to reduce the leaves and twigs to humus essential to the fertility of the soil: Woodlice, Centipedes and Millipedes, and all sorts of other little creatures in all stages of development, and, of course, the Wood Ants building their prodigious nests. In pinewoods they can be as much as three or four feet tall and twice as wide, looking as though a tidy forester had been sweeping up the dead needles. The list is endless, the activity feverish and the benefit that the forest derives from its multitude of insect inhabitants is beyond compare.

SCIENTIFIC NAMES OF INSECTS MENTIONED

Green Oak Roller Moth	*Tortrix viridana*	Brimstone	*Gonepteryx rhamni*
Mottled Umber	*Erannis defoliaria*	Red Admiral	*Vanessa atalanta*
Winter Moth	*Operophtera brumata*	Silver-washed Fritillary	*Argynnis paphia*
Oak Beauty	*Biston striataria*	Gall Wasps	*Cynips* spp.
Peppered Moth	*Biston betularia*	White Admiral	*Ladoga camilla*
Pine Beauty	*Pandlis flammea*	Pine Sawfly	*Lophyrus pini*
November Moth	*Oporinia dilutata*	Pine-shoot Beetle	*Myelophilus piniperda*
Lobster Moth	*Stauropus fagi*	Pine Weevil	*Hylobius abietis*
Goat Moth	*Cossus cossus*	Elm Bark Beetle	*Scolytus scolytus*
Purple Hairstreak	*Quercusia quercus*	Wood Ant	*Formica rufa*
Speckled Wood	*Lasiommata aegeria*		

WOODLAND BIRDS

For most of our common garden birds woodland is, or was in olden times, the natural home. The gradual disappearance of our vast natural forests has resulted in many birds extending their range outside the immediate protection of the woods, to feed in fields, orchards and open spaces, even amongst the houses in towns and cities; but most of them still need the protection of trees or shrubs in which to nest and bring up their young. Even though many thrushes, blackbirds and robins may live permanently in urban gardens, and tits may frequent the bird-tables all winter, and nest in garden boxes in the spring, the majority of all these birds live out their lives in or on the margins of woodland. And, of course, there are also a great many more rarer, shyer

species which never venture into the new, man-made environments. So, woodlands remain essential to the well-being, even vital to the existence, of most of our birds. Food, shelter and nesting sites the trees provide in plenty, whilst the birds consume prodigious quantities of insects in all their stages of development. A single pair of warblers, for instance, will bring caterpillars and other grubs to their nestful of hungry young at the rate of one a minute, destroying in the process about six hundred potential tree enemies in the course of one long summer day; and as there will probably be up to six pairs of nesting birds in every acre of woodland, the value of this insect control is significant indeed. Nor does it stop during

the rest of the year; in fact, it may be even more significant in the wintertime, for many woodland birds seek out the pupae and the hibernating adult insects and thus reduce the next year's breeding stock.

Although some woodland birds have not adapted themselves to the more open habitats of modern farms and gardens, they have to a surprising degree become accustomed to the changed environment of the modern forestry plantation, and although broadleaved woodland is still the most popular habitat, plantations with a considerable proportion of conifers attract a great many birds, far more than if there was no woodland at all. This is borne out by records which show a very considerable increase in bird life following

the establishing of conifer plantations on previously open moorland, even though the species may be different. The mere fencing in of the area to be planted causes an immediate increase in the bird population as more food and shelter is available in the grass and rushes now beyond the reach of grazing sheep, and the larks, the pipits and the plovers find life easier and safer. The fencing posts become the essential perches for some species, such as whinchats, which will not breed unless they can proclaim their territorial interests from such elevated stances. Into the new grassy oasis come masses of voles and in their wake, to feed upon them, short-eared owls. As the little trees grow up, the moorland birds leave, and the linnets, redpolls, robins, wrens and some warblers, not seen there since the old forest cover was removed centuries before, arrive attracted by the increasingly impenetrable cover provided by the fast-growing trees, which, when they reach twenty feet or so, also attract the thrushes, blackbirds and wood pigeons. As thinning starts and the lower branches

Whinchats often breed amongst recently planted conifers

Crossbills feed and breed in conifer plantations

are pruned or die away the wood becomes more open and many birds depart, perhaps disturbed by the influx of jays, magpies and crows which prefer the larger trees. After the final thinning the open woodland, though pleasant to look at and walk in, attracts few breeding birds except the ever-present goldcrest and some of the rarer hawks such as buzzards. Flocks of crossbills and other finches feed in the tall, evergreen crowns during the winter months. It is interesting to note that, of all conifer plantations, those of the introduced spruces, rather than the native pines or the deciduous larches, attract the largest number of breeding birds; indeed, a spruce plantation situated within a mature beech forest, where the shrub layer is scanty, will contain far more breeding birds per acre than there are in the beeches.

Winter and early spring, when the trees are leafless, are the best times for actually seeing birds in our woodlands, although the number of species will be fewer than after the arrival of the summer visitors. On sunny days in February the big, heavily-spotted Mistle Thrush will be singing in short, staccato phrases from the top of a tall tree and the urge to start nest-building will already be upon him and his mate; the beautiful mellow notes of the orange-billed Blackbird will drift across the rides on the warmer evenings, and the repetitious song snatches of the Song Thrush can be heard now and again all day. The Robin's sad little tinkling song comes from a patch of bushes and the Great Tit, yellow-fronted with a central black stripe, calls 'teacher teacher' from the tallest trees. A pair of Bullfinches, pink and grey, would be almost invisible as they flit in undulating flight with piping calls along the rideside, were it not for their flashing white rumps. Their near relative—and incidentally our commonest woodland bird—the Chaffinch, also pink but jaunty, assured and very visible, sings his quick, descending song. Amongst the woodland litter of pruned and dead branches, the tiny, brown, short-tailed Wren will be searching for spiders and gives forth long, almost deafening trills of song remarkable in volume for so small a bird. Sudden and startling is the clatter of a frightened Wood Pigeon as it flaps through the branches of an isolated conifer where it could have stayed had it the nerve to remain, as has the Tawny Owl which, brown, still and silent, spends the whole day pressed against a tree trunk, watchful with pivoting head and blinking, golden eyes. Sometimes he is spotted by smaller birds and will suffer their frenzied, panicky mobbing with apparent indifference.

High up in the crowns of special groups of trees, chosen who knows why, Rooks will be cawing loudly as they start to repair their nests which even the fiercest gales have failed to dislodge, and little flocks of the smaller, black Jackdaws will break up temporarily for short investigations of tree holes as possible nesting sites. A sound like calico being ripped along its length denotes the presence of the brightly coloured Jay as he drops the acorn he was about to swallow whole and sneaks away with white rump flashing. With a weird, laughing cry the Green Woodpecker, his red crown

Rooks rebuild or repair their nests in the same trees year after year

glowing, will make off with heavy undulating flight from the anthill where he was feeding with long, searching tongue, to hang on a tree trunk with gravely nodding head. The smaller, black-and-white Great Spotted Woodpecker rarely comes to the ground (although sometimes to bird-tables) but crawls up and round the tree trunks and branches in search of bugs and beetles. Neither the loud, far-reaching drumming of this bird nor the ringing, metallic cries of the grey-and-pink Nuthatch as it creeps along the upper branches of the taller trees will be heard until April. Scarcely ever to be heard is the little Tree Creeper, brown with paler breast, spending a busy day creeping up one tree to flit down to the base of another in constant search for insects in the bark crevices. And you will

The great spotted woodpecker nests in holes in trees

The brown, mouse-like treecreeper searches the bark constantly for insects as it climbs up the bole

need very keen ears indeed to pick up the thin, high-pitched twittering of the tiny, greeny Goldcrest, Britain' smallest bird, high up in the spruce branches searching diligently for insects. Later it will build a mossy nest suspended on spiders' webs and lay up to ten minute eggs.

As spring advances and March gives way to April, two little, pale-green warblers will arrive in our woods from Africa. Although the Chiffchaff and the Willow Warbler look very much alike (the former has black legs and the latter pale-brown), their songs are quite different. The chiffchaff calls its name repeatedly from high up in the trees, whilst the willow warbler lets fall its sweet, sad, cascading song from the hazel shrubs and bramble clumps. Later in the month the larger, aptly named Blackcap arrives to fill the woods with a hasty, bubbling song, and from the tall crowns, particularly of beech trees, the yellowish little Wood Warbler sings a shivering trill. In woodlands south of a line from the Severn to the Wash the rich, loud musical notes of the secretive, brown Nightingale may come pouring from the thickets.

The tiny goldcrest often hangs its nest in the branches of spruce trees

The secretive, brown nightingale is more likely to be heard than seen

The pied flycatcher is a summer visitor to the oakwoods

In May along the woodland edges a small brown bird will dart out from a branch, pick an insect out of the air, and return to its branch, repeating the process again and again—the Spotted Flycatcher. With similar habits, but rarely returning to the same branch after capturing its prey, is the distinctive black-and-white Pied Flycatcher—a charming summer inhabitant of western oakwoods where it takes very kindly to nesting boxes put up for its benefit.

By midsummer the woodland bird population reaches its peak. Many of our resident birds are sitting on their second nests and the summer visitors are all enjoying the long, insect-hunting days for which they have travelled so far to ensure food enough for their

young. For several weeks the woods have resounded to a chorus of songs, as each pair has staked its territorial claim, with the monotonous call of the Cuckoo, somehow so much part of our summer sounds, coming from the fields beyond. Gradually a silence descends. As nestlings leave the nests, the pairs break up; they have no further need to defend a territory in which to forage for their young and they cease to sing. Some will moult and set out again for Africa, others will leave the woods to claim their share of the farmers' harvest, yet others will remain skulking in the now dense undergrowth. The season of intense activity is over.

One important woodland bird we have not mentioned is the Pheasant, for it is an immigrant from western Asia and is often present in artificially large numbers on the sporting estates, especially in the early autumn before the shooting season starts. Nevertheless, it has been with us for a long time and is quite naturalised. The strident double crowing of the brightly coloured, long-tailed male, often followed by a whirring of its wings, is a very typical woodland sound, and the money earned by woodland estates from shooting rents often helps the owners to continue planting hardwoods when, without such income, only conifers would be an economic crop.

SCIENTIFIC NAMES OF BIRDS MENTIONED

Lark	*Alauda arvensis*	Tawny Owl	*Strix aluco*
Pipit	*Anthus pratensis*	Rook	*Corvus frugilegus*
Plover	*Vanellus vanellus*	Jackdaw	*Corvus monedula*
Whinchat	*Saxicola rubetra*	Jay	*Garrulus glandarius*
Robin	*Erithecus rubecula*	Green	*Picus viridis*
Linnet	*Acanthis cannabina*	Woodpecker	
Magpie	*Pica pica*	Nuthatch	*Sitta europaea*
Crow	*Corvus corone*	Tree Creeper	*Certhia familiaris*
Buzzard	*Buteo buteo*	Goldcrest	*Regulus regulus*
Crossbill	*Loxia curvirostra*	Chiffchaff	*Phylloscopus collybita*
Mistle Thrush	*Turdus viscivorus*	Willow Warbler	*Phylloscopus trochilis*
Blackbird	*Turdus merula*	Blackcap	*Sylvia atrocapilla*
Song Thrush	*Turdus philomelos*	Nightingale	*Luscinia megarhynchos*
Great Tit	*Parus major*	Spotted Flycatcher	*Muscicapa striata*
Bullfinch	*Pyrrhula pyrrhula*	Pied Flycatcher	*Ficedula hypoleuca*
Chaffinch	*Fringilla coelebs*	Cuckoo	*Cuculus canorus*
Wren	*Troglodytes troglodytes*	Pheasant	*Phasianus colchicus*
Wood Pigeon	*Columba palumbus*		

WOODLAND ANIMALS

Although the term animal includes all living things, other than those of the vegetable kingdom, from man to unicellular organisms, in this chapter we use it in the generally accepted sense to embrace only the warm-blooded mammals—those animals that give birth to live young which they suckle in the early stages of their independent existence.

There are only about fifty species of land mammals living wild in Britain and this number, with a few but important introductions by man, is substantially the same as was present when the land bridge with Europe was severed. Only the beaver, the bear, the wolf and the wild boar have been exterminated during historic times.

Unlike many insects and most birds which are frequently to be seen or heard, our animals are rarely noticed although some of them are extremely numerous. For instance, at certain times of the year there are as many field mice as there are human beings. But they are hardly ever seen, for, like most of our animals, they are essentially woodland creatures relying upon the trees and their undergrowth for concealment from their enemies. The chief of these is, in the case of the larger species, man, and in that of the smaller ones, other carnivorous animals and predatory birds.

In the natural forest, when man himself was just another hunting animal, the balance between the species was maintained; but ever since he exterminated some species and introduced others imbalances have occurred and will occur again, punctuated by periods when a certain somewhat artificial equilibrium is established. For instance, by exterminating the wolf, man removed the natural enemy of the deer, but at the same time he destroyed the forests, depriving the deer of their natural habitat, so their numbers have never got out of control. The rabbit population, at one time immense and a serious threat to agriculture and forestry because many of their natural enemies—predatory birds, stoats and weasels—had been decimated by man, has now been reduced to manageable proportions by the introduction and artificial spread of the disease myxomatosis throughout the country. Rats and mice,

Red deer stags come out to feed on the edge of the forest

similarly relieved of their natural enemies and provided by man with new environments to which they quickly adapted, occasionally reached epidemic numbers but have now been brought under control by sophisticated selective poisons.

In general today our woodland animals live in a state of reasonable equilibrium. The big herbivores, the deer, although increasing, are as yet but a very local threat to their habitat. The rodents—the voles, the wood mice, the rabbits—all fall victims to the foxes, stoats, weasels and hawks in sufficient numbers to prevent serious damage; and the insect-eaters—bats, shrews and hedgehogs—find sufficient food to maintain their numbers, doing little damage to anyone. Only one serious threat to our woodlands from an animal has yet to be met—from the introduced American Grey Squirrel. This adaptable and prolific creature, as will be seen later, is doing immense damage to many of our native broadleaved trees and with few enemies to check its numbers is driving our native red squirrel from the land.

Of all our woodland animals deer are the largest and the loveliest, with a very special fascination. The thrill of seeing a stag alert for danger on the woodland edge or of a fleeting glimpse of a buck as it melts into the deep undergrowth is never dimmed by repetition. Luckily the expansion of our forest area since the war has served the deer well and they are on the increase. The largest, the Red Deer, standing four feet at the shoulder, previously driven from its natural woodland habitat to the bare mountains of Scotland and preserved there for stalking, is now returning to our woods. The little Roe Deer finds the new conifer plantations much to its liking and is a great deal more numerous than its rather rare appearances in the open suggest. The Fallow Deer, with its flattened antlers and its spotted back, was introduced by the Normans and is now quite common in a wild state in southern England as well as being the main species kept in the deer parks of our stately homes. Even the Sika, resembling a small edition of the red deer, introduced from Japan in recent times, has spread to most parts of the country and is quite common in the south. The little Muntjac or Barking Deer, standing barely eighteen inches tall, escaped from captivity at Woburn and can now be heard, but rarely seen, barking in the beechwoods of south-east England from which it emerges at night to eat the rose bushes in nearby gardens.

Although now quite rare in some places but returning in increasing numbers in others, rabbits until the 1950s swarmed in countless numbers throughout our woodlands and were the trees' deadliest foes. Few seedlings escaped their busy teeth, and neither man, fox, stoat nor hawk could cope with their phenomenal rate of increase. Yet, these little, furry animals with their long ears and their white cottonwool tails were held in considerable if misplaced affection. Indeed, in Norman times when they were introduced, they were a valuable source of food and fur, and were farmed in warrens. But a return to the plague of them which afflicted the land before myxomatosis would be disastrous to our expanding woodlands.

Less popular in the public

The little woodmice have whiter fronts and longer tails than the house mice

eye are the mice. Two species live in our woodlands: the Wood Mouse, a pretty little creature differing from the common house mouse in having a white front, reddish-brown upper parts and a proportionately longer tail; and the Yellow-necked Mouse, larger than either with a circle of yellow fur round its neck. These mice do little damage, eating nuts, fruit and the young shoots of ground plants, and forming an important food source for the larger carnivorous animals and birds. Much more destructive is the Short-tailed Field Vole, a little mouse-like animal with a short, stubby nose, which resorts to the woods after the harvest and seriously damages small trees by eating their basal bark. Its powers of reproduction are colossal—a single pair can produce ten thousand descendants in the course of a single year—and plagues occur from time to time, but they are usually very local and well within the powers of owls and other predators to control.

With bushy tail and tufted ears, and its engaging habit of holding nuts and fir-cones in its forepaws whilst gnawing at them, the Red Squirrel has a high place in public affection which its increasing rarity does little to diminish. This delightful little animal, so typical of our woodlands, is now found wild in any numbers only in East Anglia, the extreme north of England and in Scotland. Elsewhere it appears to have been driven away by the immigrant Grey Squirrel, a much less attractive and extremely destructive creature which seems to be as much at home in parks and gardens as in the woods. At certain times of the year it plays havoc amongst hardwood trees, especially beech and sycamore, by stripping off the bark, killing saplings and ringing the upper branches of mature trees, causing disfigurement and serious damage to the timber. The feeding of these 'tree rats' during the winter months in urban parks and gardens should be discouraged, for they are a real menace to our native trees.

The animals mentioned so far have been mainly vegetarian, living on roots, shoots, nuts and fruits, but there is a group of insect-eating animals which has an important place in the woodland economy. The largest of them is the Hedgehog, rarely seen because of its nocturnal habits. Throughout the warmer months it feeds voraciously on worms, slugs and snails, as well as frogs and sometimes even eggs of ground-nesting birds, but as winter approaches it seeks out a dry spot amongst dead leaves under an old tree trunk or some such place, rolls itself up into a ball and hibernates until the spring. The tiny mouse-like Shrew, with its pointed nose and short tapering tail, is another insect-eater with a tremendous appetite, scuttling amongst the leaves and wood-litter in a feverish search for worms and any insects detected by its searching little snout. Evidence of Moles is often to be seen at the ridesides and along the woodland edges, where these subterranean creatures force up piles of earth with their immensely powerful front paws from their intricate network of burrows, where they live out their lives in total darkness and a constant search for worms.

Curiously repulsive to many people but fascinating in their powers of flight on their stretched-skin wings and in

The destructive American grey squirrel has in many areas replaced our attractive native red squirrel

their 'radar' system which enables them to catch their insect prey in darkness without colliding with tree branches, are the bats. The commonest among Britain's twelve species is the Pipistrelle which is as much at home in open country and towns as it is in the woods, where it lives in holes in old trees, emerging in the evenings to flit about in search of gnats, midges and flies which it catches on the wing. Much larger, and mainly confined to southern areas, is the Noctule which flies high and swiftly above the trees and tends to take larger insects such as beetles. Unlike the pipstrelle, it is seldom seen far from woodlands but like all bats it goes into semi-hibernation in the winter, only emerging from its tree hole on the warmest of the long dark nights.

The noctule, our largest bat, spends the day in holes or cracks in trees

The flesh-eating animals of our woods are at once beneficial in that they devour great numbers of rabbits, mice and voles, and destructive in the indiscriminate way in which they eat the eggs and young of many birds. The long, low, chestnut-brown, sinuous Stoat is a most tenacious hunter, wearing down the largest of rabbits in an unrelenting chase above and below ground, despatching its victim with a quick bite through the neck with its needle-sharp teeth; and the smaller, brown Weasel will similarly hunt down rats and mice, following their trails through the densest of undergrowth and dashing across the woodland rides with its little stubby tail held high.

Rare, but increasing as the new coniferous woodlands grow up, is the rufous, white-fronted Pine Marten which lives entirely in trees, leaping

97

Although mainly arboreal in its habits, the pine marten often has its den amongst rocks and boulders

household tabby in colour but is larger and has a fatter tail with a blunt end. It is entirely carnivorous, eating roe deer fawns, lambs, hares, rabbits and grouse, and has thus since early times been at odds with man—hence its rarity.

Although it may sometimes breed and often hunt outside the woods, the Fox needs the sanctuary of the trees in which to lie hidden during daylight hours, for it is essentially a nocturnal animal hunting alone under the stars. Beautiful and dog-like, and of legendary

from one to the next in search of squirrels and birds which it stalks cat-like along the branches. Also increasing and in some parts of west Wales now quite numerous, is the Polecat, a ferret-like animal with yellowish under-fur overlaid with long, glossy brown hairs. It is a bloodthirsty creature, killing much more than it can devour, and has thus always been an enemy of

the gamekeeper and the poultry farmer and, together with the pine marten, was once hunted almost to extinction.

Although very rare and confined to the pinewoods of the Scottish Highlands, the Wild Cat, because of the widespread affection in which its domestic cousins are held, has always attracted much public interest. Fierce and untameable, it resembles the

The wild cat is a fierce predator, still rare but increasing as our forests expand

An alert pair of fox cubs at the mouth of their earth

cunning, the fox is seldom seen; but those rare glimpses as it stands at the rideside, ears erect and one forepaw slightly raised, before melting into the undergrowth, never fail to thrill. At night, especially early in the year, the staccato bark of the dog-fox and the answering eerie wails of the vixen are wonderfully wild sounds. Destructive though it is to poultry and pheasants, most people hold this slit-eyed, bushy-tailed, sleek red animal in considerable respect and would regret its extinction; its own cunning and adaptability, and its place in the traditional chase, make this unlikely.

The Badger, grizzly grey all over, except for a black-and-white striped head and black paws, is exclusively a nocturnal animal, rarely to be seen except by the most patient of observers or as a chance glimpse in the headlights of a car. It is extremely wary about emerging from its underground labyrinth of burrows or 'sett', but once in the open it travels along much-used tracks with little attempt at concealing its ungainly progress. Worms, grubs, wasps' nests, litters of mice and rabbits are all found by chance as it snuffles and roots about beneath the trees, for it is too clumsy a creature to hunt in pursuit like a fox or a stoat. Baited as a sport in days of old, the badger now has little to fear from man or anything else, although recent evidence of a connection between it and the spread of bovine TB has resulted in its deliberate destruction in one small area. We can but hope that widespread action against these attractive and generally harmless woodland animals will not become necessary.

The black and white head of the badger shows up when it emerges from its sett at dusk

SCIENTIFIC NAMES OF ANIMALS MENTIONED

Red Deer	*Cervus elaphus*	Grey Squirrel	*Sciurus carolinensis*
Roe Deer	*Capreolus capreolus*	Hedgehog	*Erinaceus europaeus*
Fallow Deer	*Dama dama*	Shrew	*Sorex araneus*
Sika	*Sika nippon*	Mole	*Talpa europaea*
Muntjac	*Muntiacus muntjak*	Pipistrelle	*Pipistrellus pipistrellus*
Rabbit	*Oryctolagus cuniculus*	Noctule	*Nyctalus noctula*
Wood Mouse	*Apodemus sylvaticus sylvaticus*	Stoat	*Mustela erminea stabilis*
		Weasel	*Mustela nivalis nivalis*
Yellow-necked Mouse	*Apodemus flavicollis*	Pine Marten	*Martes martes martes*
		Polecat	*Mustela putorius putorius*
Short-tailed Field Vole	*Microtus agrestis*	Wild Cat	*Felis sylvestris*
		Fox	*Vulpes vulpes crucigera*
Red Squirrel	*Sciurus vulgaris*	Badger	*Meles meles meles*

VISITING WOODLANDS AND FORESTS

There are now more woodlands and forests in Britain than there have been for centuries. Although they have been planted both by the state and by private owners with the primary object of growing timber, this aim does not preclude them from being, or becoming as they grow up, places of beauty and tranquillity where people can escape from the bustle of modern life, and also refuges for wildlife. Furthermore, those planted and tended by the Forestry Commission are, in a manner of speaking, the property of the public, and the Commission encourages us all to visit them and enjoy their facilities. There are for instance throughout the country over four hundred forest walks and trails, varying in distance from a half to six miles, signposted

A forest walk through a coniferous plantation in Beddgelert Forest, North Wales

houses, cabins and chalets situated in the forests which make excellent bases from which to enjoy just the peace and quiet and the life of the woods or some of the more specialised recreational facilities. There are observation towers for watching wildlife; there is fishing on forest lakes and rivers, as well as deer-stalking and pheasant shooting; and there is pony-trekking, orienteering, sailing and canoeing.

Many owners of private woodlands, especially on the large landed estates, also allow public access and maintain

Hag Hill camp site near Reinswood, Rievaulx

at intervals and punctuated by seats placed at viewpoints. Some stretches of the ten thousand miles of forest roads have been opened up as scenic drives, showing the general scale of forestry in the area as well as giving access to the recreational facilities. More than twenty-five forest information centres have been built in which are shown, by displays and exhibits, the variety of wildlife in the forest and other features of interest. There are sixteen major camp sites for overnight and longer stays, as well as over fifty holiday

Pony trekking in Margam Forest

picnic sites, forest walks and nature trails. So, not many miles from any town or city there is likely to be woodland which you can visit, walk in and enjoy. But in doing so you take on a responsibility, a duty to help the owner and the forester to maintain that which you have come to see. The greatest danger to a forest is from fire which, in warm, dry weather, can sweep at speed through the trees, destroying humus, plants and wildlife, and at best leaving the trees weakened, maimed and unable to prosper in their new, almost lifeless habitat. Remember that a tree can make a million matches but a match can destroy a million trees.

Tree seedlings and small transplants are easily damaged and deformed for life by being trodden on, so keep to the paths and rides; in any case it is impossible to walk silently through the undergrowth and if you want to see the birds and animals you must make as little noise as possible, and what is more, very many of the woodland flowers blossom sooner and in greater numbers by the ridesides. But they are unlikely to survive uprooting

Forest fires sweep at speed through the crowns of the trees

and replanting in your garden, so leave them where they are for others to enjoy. Keep your dog under control too, for if he dashes about all over the place he will disturb deer and other animals and ground-nesting birds, especially pheasants; and although you yourself may not shoot or even approve of shooting you have no licence to spoil someone else's sport, especially if you are enjoying the hospitality of his woods. And you may find feeding hoppers for pheasant or traps for grey squirrels in the woods; here again personal feelings or curiosity should not prevent you from leaving them undisturbed.

Of course, the vast majority of woodland visitors are entirely responsible people, grateful for the opportunity to walk amongst the trees, but children cannot learn unless they are taught by example. It is well to remind ourselves and teach them our responsibility to respect the property of others as we wish them to respect ours.

An extension to the policy of giving access to Forestry Commission woodlands has been the setting up of Forest

A pheasant hatches her brood deep in the woodland undergrowth

Parks. These are areas of particularly beautiful countryside where the Commission has acquired mountainsides and open country in connection with the planting of the extensive new forests which are already in existence or are planned for the future. Access to these parks is controlled by local by-laws but, in essence, all the visitor must remember is that he should pay heed to the well-known country code which embodies much of what we have written above including, and very important, the closing of all gates and the lighting of fires or stoves only in the recognised camping sites. The parks are not only centres of the nation's important timber-growing enterprise but also include the homes of many who live by farming sheep and cattle.

There are seven such parks in all: four in Scotland, one in the Border country, one in north Wales and one straddling the county boundary between Gloucestershire and Gwent. In all of them there are well-equipped camping sites, and there are youth hostels in or near them, as well as good hotels close by. All have good

Forest parks, like this one in Snowdonia, also include hill farms and small holdings

access by road but despite this, so extensive are the stretches of moor and mountain as well as the forests themselves that it is well possible to escape from crowds and traffic to roam for hours in solitude enjoying some of our grandest scenery. The New Forest, although not officially designated as a forest park, provides similar scope for recreation and camping, even if, despite the huge area of woodland, the scenery is on a more modest scale than in the parks.

Within these parks and throughout the rest of the country are large areas of woodland in Forestry Commission hands which comprise over 180 officially named forests. These and the forest parks are listed separately, with brief details of their location and the facilities provided.

In addition to all these forests which cover more than three million acres, there are some two million acres of private woodlands, most of

them owned by members of the Royal Scottish Forestry Society and the Royal Forestry Society of England, Wales and Northern Ireland. These societies, the addresses of which are given on page 115, are able to give details of those woods which are open to the public.

These two societies hold outdoor meetings in woodlands throughout the country during the late spring, summer and early autumn, led by experts in forestry and arboriculture. These meetings, which are open to all members who receive notice of them in an annual fixture card, provide excellent opportunities for learning and for meeting other people with similar interests; and they often give entrée to places not normally open to the public.

There is much of interest to be seen in Forest Information Centres and Forest Museums such as this one at Grizedale, Cumbria

FOREST PARKS

Glenmore Forest Park

Situated in the Cairngorms on three sides of Loch Morlich, east of Aviemore; 3,600 acres of woodland, including the old Caledonian pines in the Queen's Forest, as well as mountainsides rising to the summit of Cairngorm (4,084 ft).

Argyll Forest Park

Includes the forests of Ardgartan, Glenbrantar and Benmore as well as rugged hillsides broken by sea lochs; covers in all some 62,000 acres stretching from west of Loch Eck to the western shore of Loch Lomond and from the Holy Loch to Arrochar.

Queen Elizabeth Forest Park

Stretches east from Loch Lomond to the Trossachs, covering some 42,000 acres; includes parts of Achray, Loch Ard and Buchanan Forests, the summits of Ben Lomond (3,192 ft) and Ben Venue (2,386 ft) and the shorelines of Lochs Lomond, Chon, Ard, Achray, Venacher and Drunkie.

Galloway Forest Park

Extends over 160,000 acres of Dumfries and Galloway and the southern tip of the Strathclyde Region; includes the forests of Glentrool, Kirroughtree and Clatteringshaws, as well as sixteen hill lochs, the highest hill in south Scotland, Merrick (2,764 ft), and much of the Rhinns of Kells.

Border Forest Park

Covers 145,000 acres along the Cheviots and neighbouring hills in Cumbria, Northumberland and Scotland; extends to Kershope and Newcastleton Forests in Liddesdale and Wauchope Forest west of Carter Bar, as well as the forests of Kielder, Mounces, Falstone, Wark and Redesdale in Northumberland.

Snowdonia Forest Park

Comprises 23,500 acres of woodland, moorland and lakes amidst the foothills of Snowdon (3,561 ft); it is centred on Betws-y-Coed where the wooded Llugwy Valley joins the Conway vale, and includes the forests of Gwydyr and Beddgelert.

Dean Forest Park

Includes over 32,000 acres of mixed broadleaved and coniferous forest situated round the junction of the Severn and Wye valleys in Gloucestershire and Gwent, with spectacular

As well as the forest parks listed opposite there are many other smaller forests which can be visited within easy motoring distance of the major towns and cities

Shin Forest

Torrachilty Forest

Affric Forest

Glenmore Forest Park

Bennachie Forest

Glengarry Forest

Tornashean Forest

Glenrigh Forest

Rannock Forest

Aberdeen

Glencoe and Barcaldine Forest

Tummel Forest

Dunkeld Forest

Dundee

Argyll Forest Park

Queen Elizabeth Forest Park

Knapdale Forest

Glasgow

Edinburgh

Glentress Forest

The Border Forest Park

Galloway Forest Park

Carlisle

Hamsterley Forest

Grizedale Forest

Cropton and Dalby Forest

Bradford

Leeds

Liverpool

Manchester

Sheffield

Snowdonia Forest Park

Delamere Forest

Sherwood Forest

Beddgelert Forest

Clocaenog Forest

Code-y-Brenin Forest

Nottingham

Rheidol Forest

Cannock Forest

Wyne Forest

Birmingham

Norwich

Tywi Forest

Thetford Forest

Coed Tag Fawr Forest

Aldewood Forest

Swansea

Dean Forest Park

Coed Morgannwg Forest

Ebbw Forest

Tintern Forest

Bristol

London

Savernake Forest

Alice Holt Forest

The New Forest

Southampton

Queen Elizabeth Forest Park

Plymouth

Brighton

109

scenery such as the Wye Valley Gorge and Symonds Yat Rock, as well as historic buildings in and around the Forest of Dean and Tintern Forest.

A forest caravan site beneath old oak trees in Denny Wood, New Forest

Forest workers are on the spot with their houses in Coed Gwili

BOOKS ON TREES

During the last twenty years or so a large number of books on trees has been published, most of them with the main object of assisting in identification, some designed to stimulate an interest by means of attractive photographs, and some highly specialised, concentrating in considerable detail on one or other group of trees.

It all really started in 1662 when John Evelyn read his paper *Sylva or A Discourse of Forest Trees* to the newly formed Royal Society at the request of Charles II, who had become seriously worried about the shortage of oak for the Royal Navy's ships. So impressed was his audience that Evelyn was asked to print the paper which became the basis of a book with the same title, issued as a folio volume in 1664, containing a prodigious

amount of information ranging from minor practical and personal observations to legendary classical allusions on matters concerning trees that could or might be grown in Britain. Four subsequent editions were published in 1670, 1679 and 1706, the year Evelyn died; but even then it was not finished. In 1776 a Scots doctor, Alexander Hunter, produced a new edition, heavily annotated, the notes being of considerable interest. Further editions of this were published in 1786, 1801 and 1812.

Copies of the four original Evelyn editions are hard to come by, but Hunter's revisions are sometimes to be found in bookshops, and are certainly available from good public libraries. To those who wish to trace the history of British

forestry practice and the woodlands which resulted from it, as well as the build-up of practical knowledge about the cultivation of forest trees, this book is of tremendous interest.

Encouraged, no doubt, by the interest in tree-planting which the success of Evelyn's work had shown, J. C. Loudon, an eminent horticulturalist who had already published his *Encyclopaedia of Gardening* in 1827, decided to bring up to date and enlarge upon the *Sylva* with the 'hope of diffusing more generally, among gentlemen of landed property, a taste for introducing a greater variety of trees and shrubs in their plantations and pleasure gardens'. In 1834 he sent out three thousand proformas to landowners, foresters, nurserymen, gardeners and amateur enthusiasts in

Britain, America and Europe, listing all the known genera of trees and shrubs hardy in temperate climates, and asking for details of age, size, shape, situation of specimens known to them. With the information thus supplied by his correspondents, and from his own profound knowledge and experience, he wrote the monumental, eight-volume work *Arboretum et Fruticetum Britannicum* which was first published in 1838. It was the first complete treatise on trees and shrubs, native and introduced, which 'endure the open air in Britain'. The first four volumes contain a geographical and historical survey together with individual description of trees and shrubs, illustrated with 2,546 engravings, and notes on their uses, propagation and culture, as well as, and of especial interest, particulars of the location and statistics of size and shape of individual trees up and down the country. The last four volumes contain 412 engraved portraits of trees and shrubs, nearly all taken from specimens growing at that time within ten miles of London.

Of course, advances in botanical knowledge since then, and the discovery of many more trees in various parts of the world, have resulted in name changes, reclassifications and increases to nearly all the families described by Loudon. Nevertheless the work is a masterpiece, still of the greatest interest and by no means totally outdated. Its immediate effect was amply to justify the author's hopes. At a time when forestry was in a decline, as we have seen, an enthusiasm for collecting and planting specimen and amenity trees was so encouraged and stimulated by Loudon that Britain became the leading nation in arboriculture, and we enjoy to this day great tree collections inspired by this remarkable man.

The original work and a shortened version (1,200 pages) called *Trees and Shrubs of Great Britain*, can still be bought in some of the larger secondhand bookshops and are available in libraries.

The advent of photography, greater ease of travel and a steady increase in the introduction of new trees from many parts of the world, persuaded two men, a Gloucestershire landowner, H. J. Elwes, and a former Chinese Customs officer become professor of forestry at Trinty College, Dublin, A. H. Henry, to combine in the production of a new book. Their *Trees of Great Britain and Ireland* was published privately, financed by subscription, and limited to five hundred copies. The first volume appeared in 1906 and was to be followed by four others. In the event, so great was the amount of information amassed and the number of new trees discovered that the work ended up as seven volumes, the last being published in 1913. It is a classic, giving a 'complete account of all the trees which grow naturally or are cultivated in Great Britain and which have attained or seem likely to attain a size which justifies their being looked on as timber trees'. It also contains four hundred photographs of individual trees taken at home and abroad, of remarkable clarity and composition, as well as identification drawings of the more difficult families; and measurement, with locations, of outstanding specimen trees

growing in this country and abroad, many of which are still to be found. Searching them out is a fascinating pastime.

Very readable for so large and detailed a book, and of impeccable authenticity, for the authors were as widely travelled as they were knowledgeable, this work remains unchallenged to this day. The original edition is so rare as to be quite beyond the means of most of us, but a reprint was published by EP Publishing, in conjunction with the Royal Forestry Society, in 1969 at £7·50 per volume.

In 1914, W. J. Bean, curator of the Royal Botanic Gardens, Kew, published his two-volume *Trees and Shrubs Hardy in the British Isles*, and a third volume was added in 1933. Subsequent and progressively more expensive editions have brought the work completely up to date. A few line drawings and a limited number of photographs accompany a concise but descriptive text making it a valuable reference book, but for sheer weight of information it cannot compare with Elwes and Henry, although it includes many more species.

For the conifer enthusiast Dallimore and Jackson's *Handbook of Coniferae and Ginkgoaceae*, published in 1923, is an exceedingly comprehensive and readable reference book, with excellent line drawings and a modicum of photographs. A new edition has recently been published.

The books mentioned so far are expensive and beyond the means of most of us, but are, of course, by no means essential to the beginner or to those whose interest in trees goes no further than a nodding acquaintance with our more common species. For them one or more of the modern books listed below will suffice. But anyone who comes under the spell of trees, and particularly those of us who have been described as having been 'bitten by a mad tree', will gain an intense and lasting pleasure from studying the early theories of Evelyn, the remarkable detail of Loudon's observations, the much-travelled authority of Elwes and Henry and their unique photographs, and the concise but comprehensive scope of Bean and Dallimore and Jackson.

British Woodland Trees, H. L. Edlin, third edition, 1949; 182 pages, 133 plates, 126 line drawings; original price 12s. 6d.

Forestry and Woodland Life, H. L. Edlin, second edition, 1948; 184 pages, 182 plates; original price 10s. 6d.

British Trees: A Guide for Everyman, Miles Hadfield, 1957; 468 pages, hundreds of line drawings; original price 30s.

Trees, Woods and Man, H. L. Edlin, New Naturalist Series, 1956; 272 pages, 48 plates (24 in colour); original price 30s.

Welsh Timber Trees, H. A. Hyde, revised edition, 1961; 173 pages, 28 plates, 53 line drawings; original price 18s.

Trees and Bushes, H. Vedel and J. Lange, 1960; 224 pages, 120 colour plates (paintings), distribution maps; original price 16s.

The International Book of Trees, Hugh Johnson, 1973; 288 pages, nearly 1,000 coloured photographs and drawings; price £9·95.

Living Trees of the World, T. H. Everett, 1969; 314 pages, 350 plates (67 in colour); price £5·25.

A Field Guide to the Trees of Britain and Northern Europe, Alan Mitchell; 415 pages, 40 coloured plates and 600 line drawings; price £2·95.

Trees and Bushes of Europe, Oleg Polunin, 1976; 208 pages, 1,000 coloured photographs and drawings; price £5·25.

Know Your Broadleaves, H. L. Edlin, Forestry Commission Booklet No. 20, 1968; 142 pages, 75 photographs and line drawings; original price 15s.

Know Your Conifers, H. L. Edlin, Forestry Commission Booklet No. 15, 1965; 56 pages, 63 photographs and line drawings; original price 5s.

Conifers in the British Isles, A. F. Mitchell, Forestry Commission Booklet No. 33, 1972; 322 pages, 24 photographs, 203 line drawings; price £2·25.

Trees of the World, Scott Leathart, 1977; 224 pages, 260 colour photographs, 120 line drawings; price £4·95.

In addition to these books, there are many Forestry Commission publications, mostly quite inexpensive, on a wide range of forestry and woodland subjects, obtainable from government bookshops in the larger cities. There are also the official publications of the Royal Scottish Forestry Society and the Royal Forestry Society of England, Wales and Northern Ireland—*Scottish Forestry* and *Quarterly Journal of Forestry*—which are issued free to members quarterly; as well as *Trees* from the Men of the Trees and *Forestry and British Timber* published by Benn Publications six times a year.

SOCIETIES CONNECTED WITH FORESTRY AND TREES

Societies Connected with Forestry and Trees

The Royal Scottish Forestry Society, 18 Abercromby Place, Edinburgh EH3 6LB (Tel. 031–557 1017).

The Royal Forestry Society of England, Wales and Northern Ireland, 102 High St, Tring, Herts., HP23 4AH (Tel. 0442–82 2028).

The Institute of Foresters of Great Britain, 6 Rutland Sq., Edinburgh EH1 2AU.

The Men of the Trees, Crawley Down, Sussex (Tel. Copthorne 712536).

The Arboricultural Association, 59 Blythewood Gardens, Stansted, Essex.

All these societies have various classes of membership and it is not necessary to have qualifications in order to join them—just an interest in trees or forestry—and all of them will send details of their aims and objects if requested.

The Forestry Commission, 231 Corstorphine Rd, Edinburgh EH12 7AT, will always give help and advice on matters connected with access to their forests.

The government-sponsored **Tree Council**, Room 202, 17/19 Rochester Row, London SW1P 1LN, can be approached for help and information on matters connected with amenity tree planting.